upgrading to
mac os x 10.4 tiger

Visual QuickProject Guide

by Tom Negrino

Peachpit
Press

Visual QuickProject Guide
Upgrading to Mac OS X 10.4 Tiger
Tom Negrino

Peachpit Press

1249 Eighth Street
Berkeley, CA 94710
510/524-2178
800/283-9444
510/524-2221 (fax)

Find us on the World Wide Web at: www.peachpit.com
To report errors, please send a note to errata@peachpit.com
Peachpit Press is a division of Pearson Education

Editor: Nancy Davis
Production: Andrei Pasternak
Compositor: WolfsonDesign
Cover design: The Visual Group with Aren Howell
Cover production: WolfsonDesign
Cover photo credit: iStockphoto.com
Interior design: Elizabeth Castro
Indexer: Rebecca Plunkett

Notice of Rights

Notice of Liability

Trademarks

ISBN 0-321-35756-6

9 8 7 6 5 4 3 2 1

Printed and bound in the United States of America

For Dori, Sean, and Pixel the Skeptical Cat
(www.pixel.mu)

Special Thanks to...

My superb editor, Nancy Davis.

The book's production editor, Andrei Pasternak, and the compositor, Owen Wolfson. Thanks for turning my laughable scratch layouts into a real book.

As always, my love and thanks to my family, who put up with Cranky Tom On a Deadline with mostly good cheer.

contents

contents

introduction

The Visual QuickProject Guide that you hold in your hands offers a unique way to learn about new technologies. Instead of drowning you in theoretical possibilities and lengthy explanations, this Visual QuickProject Guide uses big, color illustrations coupled with clear, concise step-by-step instructions to show you how to complete one specific project in a matter of hours.

Our project in this book is to upgrade to Mac OS X 10.4, also known by its code-name, Tiger. We will properly prepare for the upgrade by making sure you have what you need and by backing up your hard drive, then we'll dive into the upgrade itself. After the upgrade, we'll learn how to customize your system for maximum utility, and learn about Tiger's new features, including the big three new features: Spotlight, Dashboard, and Automator.

how this book works

The title of each section explains what is covered on that page.

build a workflow (cont.)

3 Now we'll add an action that finds the iTMS songs. Click the Spotlight entry in the Library column, then drag Find iTunes Items from the Action column to the workflow area, below the Ask for Confirmation action. In the Find pop-up menu, choose Songs. In the Whose section, choose Kind from the first pop-up menu, choose Contains from the second pop-up menu, and type Protected in the text field (songs bought from the iTMS have the kind MPEG-4 Audio File (Protected)).

Numbered steps explain actions to perform in a specific order.

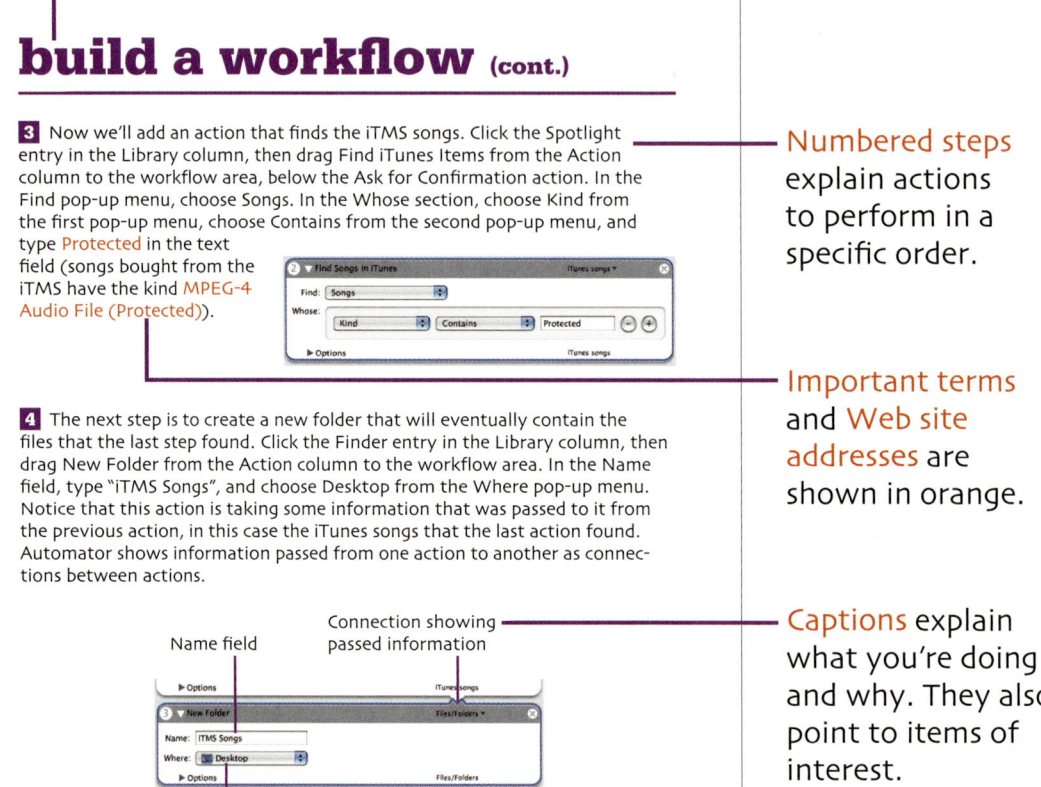

Important terms and Web site addresses are shown in orange.

4 The next step is to create a new folder that will eventually contain the files that the last step found. Click the Finder entry in the Library column, then drag New Folder from the Action column to the workflow area. In the Name field, type "iTMS Songs", and choose Desktop from the Where pop-up menu. Notice that this action is taking some information that was passed to it from the previous action, in this case the iTunes songs that the last action found. Automator shows information passed from one action to another as connections between actions.

Name field

Connection showing passed information

Captions explain what you're doing and why. They also point to items of interest.

Where pop-up menu

110   **save time with automator**

The extra bits section at the end of each chapter contains additional tips and tricks that you might like to know—but that aren't absolutely necessary for completing the upgrade and using Tiger.

extra bits

The heading for each group of tips matches the section title.

The page number next to the heading makes it easy to refer back to the main content.

check your hard disk p. 27

- In Disk Utility, you could click Verify Disk, but then it would check the hard disk, and tell you that there was a problem (if one exists), after which you would just have to click Repair Disk anyway, so you may as well cut to the chase.

- In rare cases, Disk Utility will find disk directory damage that it can't repair. In that case, I suggest that you suspend upgrading to Tiger and do two things. First, you should purchase Disk Warrior, from Alsoft (www.alsoft. com). Disk Warrior is an extra-strength utility that can rebuild a damaged disk directory. Run Disk Warrior on the damaged drive, then make another backup, then continue upgrading to Tiger. Alternatively, you could simply do an Erase and Install installation of Tiger, and allow the Setup Assistant to copy your files back to your Mac's hard drive from your backup drive. When the Installer erases the internal drive it also clears the directory damage (along with everything else on your disk).

choose upgrade type p. 28

- If you have problems with an Upgrade installation and you need to revert to your old system from your backup, I recommend that you next try an Archive and Install upgrade, then if you still have trouble, an Erase and Install installation.

- If you choose to do an Erase and Install installation, after your computer reboots into Tiger the Setup Assistant will run and offer to copy all of your personal files from another volume. If you made a backup onto another hard drive, the Setup Assistant will do most of the work of copying your files back to your main drive for you.

- Erase and Install gives you a choice of how you want to format your hard drive. Your choices are Mac OS Extended (Journaled), which is the one you should choose, or UNIX File System, which is for very specialized installations.

the next step

While this Visual QuickProject Guide will walk you through all of the steps required to upgrade to Tiger and start to use it, there's more to learn about Tiger. After you complete your QuickProject, consider picking up one of two books, also published by Peachpit, as an in-depth, handy reference.

To learn more details about every aspect of Tiger, take a look at Mac OS X 10.4 Tiger: Visual QuickStart Guide, by Maria Langer.

Once you're familiar and comfortable with Tiger, improve your skills to insane, barely-legal levels by picking up Mac OS X Tiger Killer Tips, by Scott Kelby.

Each book gives you clear examples, concise, step-by-step instructions, and many helpful tips that will vault you from newbie to power user.

1. prepare to upgrade

I know that what you really want to do is just put that Tiger disk into your Mac and get started with the upgrade. But have patience; the things that I'll be walking you through in this and the next chapter will ensure that when you do upgrade to Tiger, your upgrade will go smoothly, with a minimum of annoyances and fiddling about.

In this chapter, you'll confirm that your Mac is ready for Tiger; learn to avoid issues that could make it difficult to start up your Mac after the upgrade; and learn to disable software until you need it again after you have completed the upgrade successfully.

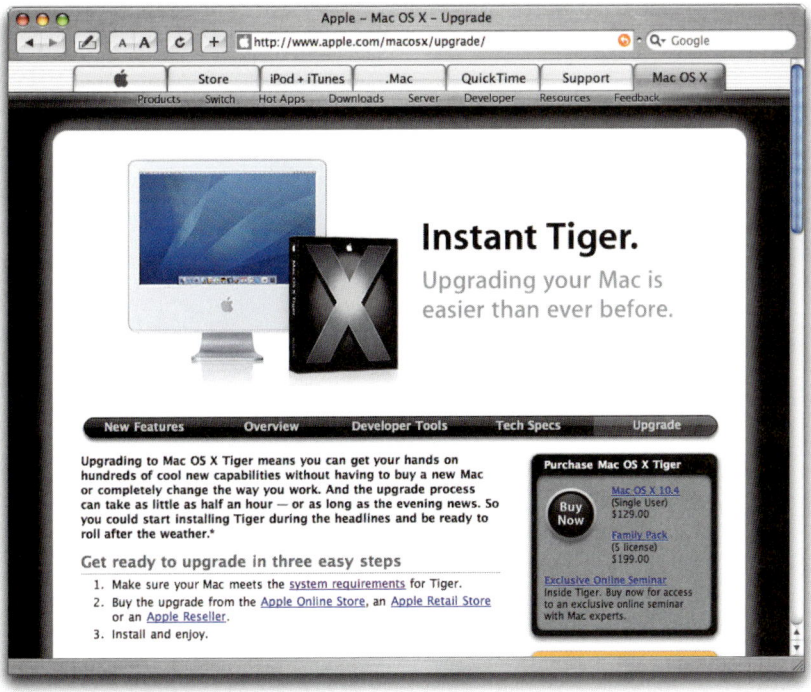

check your system

Before you install, you need to make sure that your Mac's hardware can handle Tiger. That's not too difficult; if your Mac was built in the past few years, you will almost certainly have no problems running Tiger. According to Apple, your machine requires the following to run Tiger:

- It has to have a G3, G4, or G5 processor.

- It needs at least 256 MB of RAM (Random Access Memory), though Mac OS X really needs at least 512 MB. If you have 256 MB, I strongly suggest that you consider purchasing and installing a RAM upgrade. There are too many permutations of machines and RAM configurations for me to list them all here, but it should cost you well under $50 to buy the RAM you need. Apple says that you should be able to install RAM yourself (try it, it's pretty easy), but if you need a technician to do it, your local computer store should do it for another $25 or so.

- You need at least 3 GB of available hard disk space.

- Your machine needs to have a built-in FireWire port.

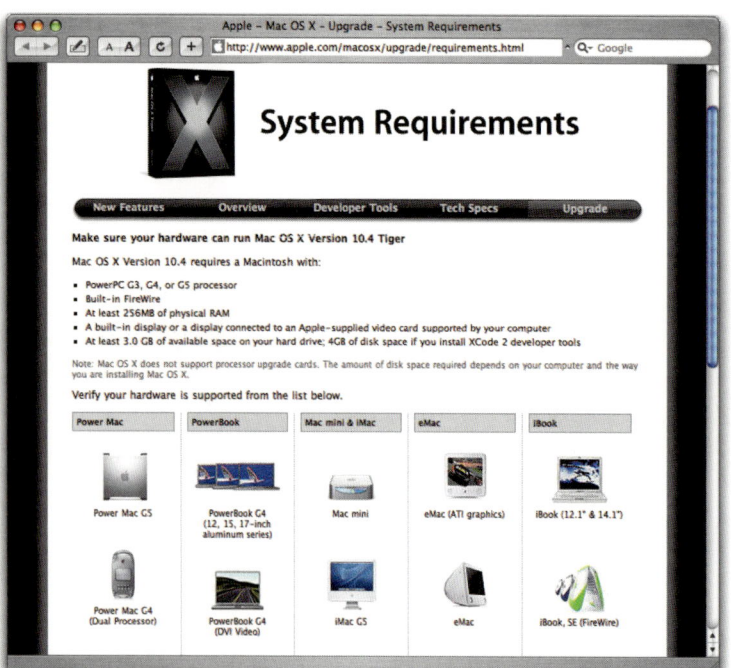

If you're not sure if your machine qualifies, take a look at the pictorial list of Macs that Apple has provided at www.apple.com/macosx/upgrade/requirements.html.

prepare to upgrade

To check to see what processor and how much RAM your Mac has, choose Apple > About This Mac. The resulting window lists the processor and installed memory.

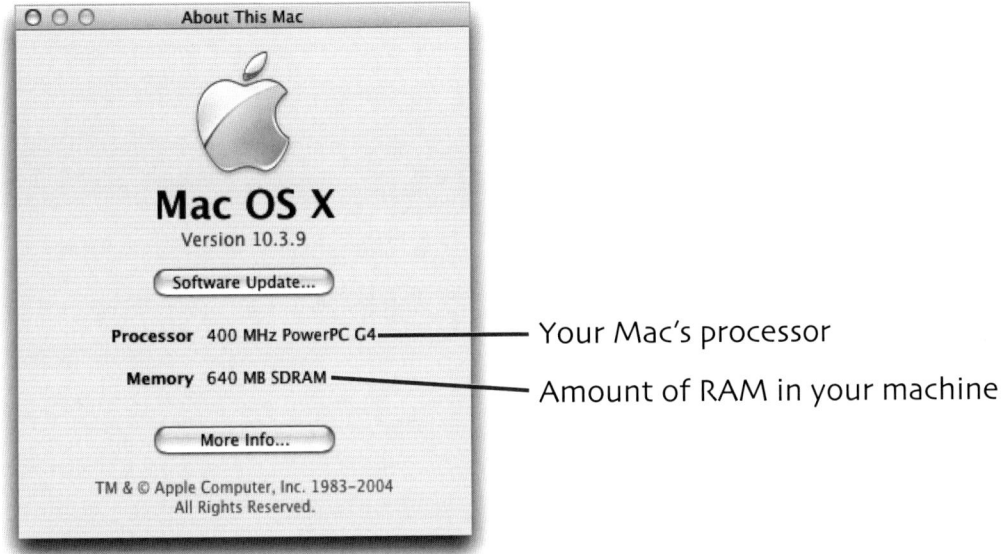

Your Mac's processor

Amount of RAM in your machine

check your system (cont.)

To tell how much disk space you have available, the easiest way is to click once on the icon of your hard disk on the desktop to select it, then choose File > Get Info. In the Get Info window, the available disk space will be listed.

Panther HD Info

▼ General:

Panther HD

Kind: Volume
Where: Desktop:
Created: Tuesday, January 25, 2005 1:50 PM
Modified: Monday, April 18, 2005 3:55 PM
Format: Mac OS Extended (Journaled)
Capacity: 9.44 GB

Available disk space ——— Available: 7.17 GB

Used: 2.27 GB on disk (2,447,011,840 bytes)

▶ Name & Extension:

▶ Content index:

▶ Preview:

▶ Ownership & Permissions:

▶ Comments:

If your available space is less than 3 GB, you'll need to move or delete files from your hard disk before you upgrade. Tiger needs a bit more disk space to install than it does to run, so after the upgrade is done, you will likely have space available for your documents. Consider getting rid of applications that you never use, or archive old documents and photos to a CD, DVD, or external hard drive. If you have an iPod, you can even move files to it temporarily.

The Apple system requirements page also says that you need "A built-in display or a display connected to an Apple-supplied video card supported by your computer." All that means is that if your Mac has a third-party video card (very few Macs do), you should check to make sure that the manufacturer has certified it for Tiger. In some cases, you may need to update the video card or its software.

prepare to upgrade

need tiger on cd?

Tiger comes on a DVD-ROM, which can be read just fine by what Apple calls "combo" drives (that's an optical drive that can read and write CDs, and read DVDs) or SuperDrives (drives that can read and write both CDs and DVDs). Chances are, your machine will be able to handle the Tiger DVD. But older Macs may have come with only a CD-ROM drive, which cannot read the Tiger DVD. Once you purchase Tiger, Apple has a Media Exchange Program that allows you to send in your Tiger DVD, a proof of purchase, and $9.95 and get Tiger on a set of CDs.

check drivers

A driver is software that enables your Mac to use a hardware device. Driver software for all the hardware that came in your Mac is built into Mac OS X, so you don't need to worry about it. It's the external hardware devices that should concern you.

The most common external device is a printer, and in this case, you're probably covered. Mac OS X includes many printer drivers that are installed when you install the system, and includes Gimp-Print, a set of open-source printer drivers. If you've been printing already on your current system, you know that your printer is supported. Otherwise, you should find a driver either written by the manufacturer (if necessary, check their Web site) or as part of the vast Gimp-Print collection.

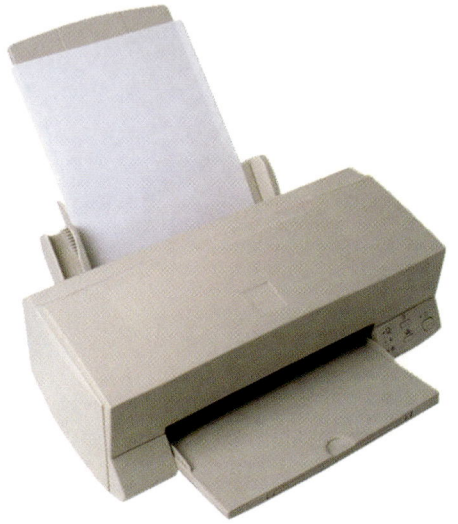

If you have a scanner, the manufacturer almost certainly provided software to work with it. Check the manufacturer's Web site for a Tiger update, though the Panther (Mac OS X 10.3) drivers should work well.

prepare to upgrade

Input devices, such as mice, trackballs, keyboards, or graphics tablets often use drivers to help you get the most out of them. Mac OS X can handle two-button mice with scroll wheels with no extra drivers needed. If your device has more buttons, it may need drivers to take advantage of them. Check the manufacturer's Web site for the latest versions of their driver software.

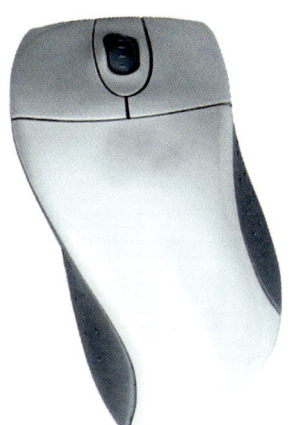

You may also need drivers for the following kinds of devices; check the manufacturer's Web site for the device to find updated versions:

- Video cards give you higher-performance graphics than was included with your Mac or simply allow you to use an additional monitor.

- Audio equipment such as a MIDI interface or digital audio interface, both used by musicians, usually runs via USB or FireWire, and often requires drivers.

check utilities

If you use any utility programs to make your computing experience easier or more pleasant, you should check to see that they are compatible with Tiger. That's especially important if the utility modifies the system in some way, or is triggered by a keyboard hotkey. A badly implemented or incompatible utility can cause your Mac to crash or not boot properly.

One example of a useful utility I've used for years is St. Clair Software's Default Folder X, which enhances the Open and Save dialogs in any Mac OS X program. It makes it much easier and faster to find files and do what you want in those dialogs.

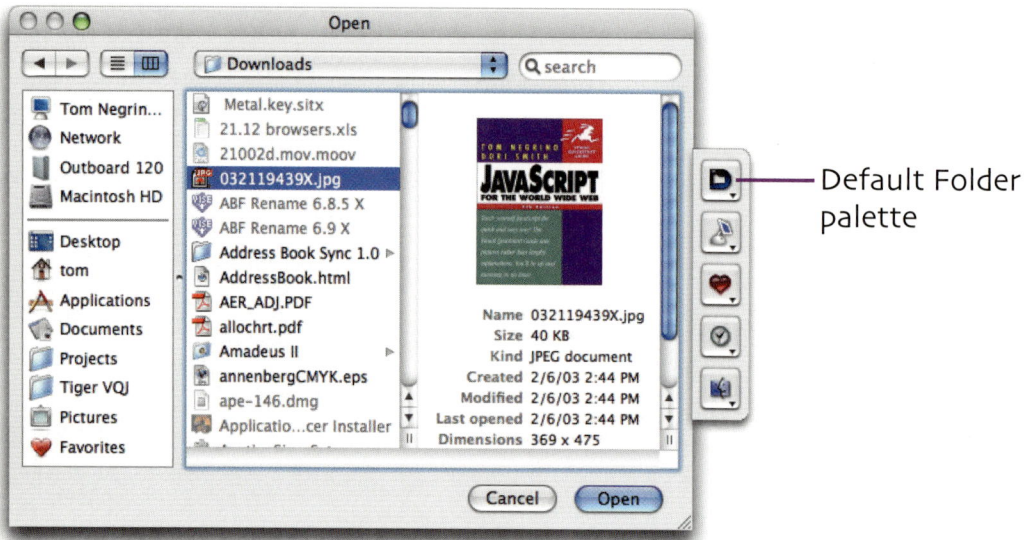

Default Folder palette

Default Folder not only enhances the system, but also lets you use hotkeys to jump to folders in an Open or Save dialog. So it interacts with the system in many ways, and it was important to make sure that it was compatible with the system before I did my upgrade to Tiger. As it turns out, the developer had an update to the program ready for Tiger's introduction.

prepare to upgrade

I suggest that you make a list of the third-party utilities (if any) that you have installed on your current system and run through the following process:

1 Do you still use the utility? Sometime I'll download a program to try it out, install it, and then decide that I don't want to continue using it, but forget to remove it. If a utility on your list falls in that category, remove it from your system before you do the Tiger upgrade. You can usually just throw the utility in the Trash to get rid of it.

2 If you're using the utility, check its Web site for the latest version. Make sure that the most recent version is Tiger-compatible. If it is, download it from the Web site, but don't install it right now; you'll do that in Chapter 4 after you do the Tiger upgrade.

3 Many utilities are made by small, independent developers, and they may have dropped support for their software since the last time you checked. If that's the case, there probably won't be a new version for Tiger. For some software, that won't be a problem; the older version may work just fine. But if there's an incompatibility, you may have to look for a replacement utility. You can often find multiple programs that do many of the same things as that orphaned utility. A good resource for finding Mac software is Version Tracker (www.versiontracker.com).

do you need OS 9?

If you've been using a Mac for several years, you may still be using a few Mac OS 9 applications. Mac OS 9 runs under Mac OS X in a compatibility mode called the Classic environment. If you're upgrading from a previous version of Mac OS X that had Mac OS 9 installed, you should still be able to use the Classic environment and Mac OS 9 applications after you upgrade to Tiger.

If you need Classic, and your machine doesn't have Mac OS 9 already installed, you'll need a Mac OS 9 install disk. Unfortunately, Apple no longer sells Mac OS 9, so you will need to find another source. I suggest that you look for a copy on eBay (www.ebay.com).

check startup items

Some software has components that run automatically when your Mac starts up. These were called Login Items in Jaguar (10.2), Startup Items in Panther (10.3), and are now called Login Items again in Tiger (10.4). When you do an upgrade to Tiger, the Tiger Installer copies the previous startup items to the new system and activates them, ready to use. This could be either good or bad. It's certainly more convenient for you. But if a startup item that was on your old system is incompatible with Tiger, your Mac could crash when it boots up. And that's just no fun at all.

That's why it is so important to make sure that your software and utilities are up-to-date before you upgrade to Tiger. It will help if you check to see what software is set as Startup Items. To find out, open System Preferences, then click Accounts.

If there is more than one account on your machine, click your account in the column on the left, then click the Startup Items tab, as shown here for Panther.

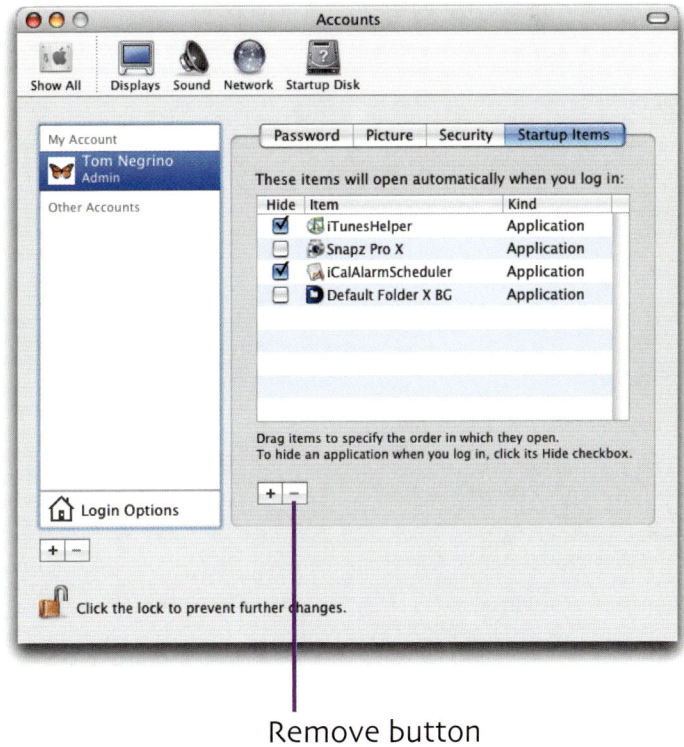

Remove button

check startup items (cont.)

You should not be concerned about items that are associated with Apple applications, as they are either updated with Tiger, compatible with Tiger, or both. If there is an item that is not from Apple, however, you should check to see what version it is, and then look for a possible update on the product's Web site.

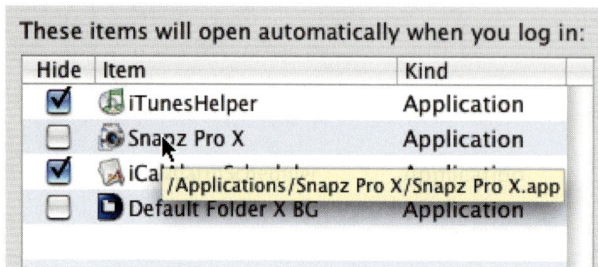

To see where to find the item, hover the cursor over its name and a tip window appears with the path to the item.

Find the item on your hard disk, click once to select it, then choose File > Get Info. In the Info window, note the version number of the item.

Version number

Write down the version number, then check the product's Web site. If there is a later version, go back to the Startup Items window, select the item in the list, and click the Remove button. That way the older version won't be brought over to Tiger when you do the upgrade. You should also download the newer version from the product's Web site, but don't install it yet. For safety's sake, we'll install it after the upgrade.

prepare to upgrade

extra bits

check your system p. 2

- If you need to get a RAM upgrade for your Mac, Ramseeker (www.ramseeker.com) is an excellent source to find good mail order prices.

- Memory is fairly easy to install yourself, and Apple has handy installation instructions on their Web site at www.info.apple.com/usen/cip/.

- If you have an older Mac that doesn't have a built-in FireWire port, you may not be able to upgrade to Tiger; just putting in a FireWire card won't work, because the Installer will not run. However, there is a workaround for some machines called XPost-Facto (http://eshop.macsales.com/OSXCenter/XPostFacto/). This software helps Mac OS X work on some older machines. Apple doesn't support the workaround, so you're on your own to get it up and running.

- Tiger says farewell to some older Macs, which are not supported, such as the early iMacs and the "Lombard" G3 Power-Books. Again, XPostFacto may help you get Tiger running, but you should consider when to let go of a machine that's more than five years old and get something

newer. Performance will certainly suffer on older machines, because Tiger is processor, memory, and graphics intensive. Personally, my advice is that if your Mac has a G3 processor, or a G4 that's slower than about 600 MHz, you sell it or donate it to a good cause and purchase a newer machine.

check drivers p. 6

- Tiger installs printer drivers for printers from the following manufacturers: Brother, Canon, Electronics for Imaging, Epson, Hewlett-Packard, Lexmark, Ricoh, and Xerox.

- When choosing a printer driver, it's usually a better idea to use a driver written by the printer's manufacturer, if available, rather than using one of the Gimp-Print open source drivers. Drivers made by the printer manufacturers are generally higher quality and offer more detailed functionality than an open-source driver. The nice thing about the Gimp-Print drivers is that they cover many older printers for which the manufacturers might not have Mac OS X drivers.

continues on next page

extra bits

- You can get a quick productivity boost by ditching the one-button Apple mouse and getting a multiple-button mouse with a scroll wheel. It makes using the Mac ever so much more efficient. I use a Microsoft Intellimouse Explorer with four buttons and a scroll wheel, and it lets me navigate through the Finder, scroll windows, and cruise through Web sites much faster. Kensington and Logitech also make good mice and trackballs.

- With a multiple-button mouse, clicking the right mouse button is the same as Control-clicking with a one-button mouse. It allows you to bring up contextual menus in virtually all applications.

check utilities p. 8

- Check out my pick of the best utilities for Mac OS X in Chapter 10.

prepare to upgrade

2. **back it up!**

Stop right there! Don't turn past this chapter!

Let me be perfectly clear: if you don't back up your computer before you upgrade to Tiger, you're practically asking for trouble. While most upgrades go smoothly, in some cases an upgrade can go horribly wrong, leaving you without a working Mac. And Murphy's Law says that it's going to happen to you, if you don't back up your computer first. The documents you've built up over the years are precious, and very few among us can afford the time and trouble to recreate all of our files from scratch, even if it were possible. You Have Been Warned.

While you should be doing regular backups to guard against hardware failure, theft, volcanic eruptions, extraterrestrial attack, and other nightmares, this chapter will focus on creating a single safety backup that will save your files (and your bacon) in the event of disaster. It's easy to do, not very expensive, and you'll sleep better when you've gotten it done. Plus, you'll have a backup system in place for periodic backups.

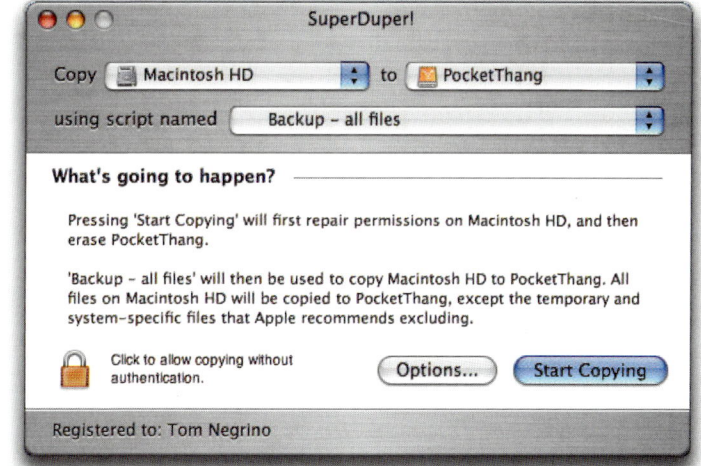

choose backup tools

Backing up is the process of copying some or all of the files and folders on your hard disk to another storage medium. You need two things to back up: hardware and software. For the hardware, you have a choice of backup media, but I'm only going to discuss two of them.

If you have a SuperDrive in your Mac, you can burn files to a recordable DVD. The good news is that a DVD holds 4.7 GB. That's the bad news, too, because the average size hard disk in a new Mac is 80 GB. Most people don't have their whole hard disk filled up, but even 40 GB of data (and it's not hard to amass that with the help of iTunes, iPhoto, and iMovie) is more DVDs than you want to record. It also takes a significant amount of time to burn a whole DVD, as much as half an hour. Burning files to a DVD is fine if you are only backing up a relatively small amount of data, little enough so that it will fit on a single DVD.

For sufficient protection before a system upgrade, you'll need an external FireWire hard drive. An external hard drive that connects via FireWire is surprisingly inexpensive (in early 2005, I put together a new backup system built around two external 160 GB drives that cost $95 apiece), fast, and can back up the entire contents of your computer (called a duplicate or clone backup) before your Tiger upgrade. You can then use it to continue backing up your computer on a regular schedule. These drives are the way to go. I suggest that you purchase a drive that has a capacity of at least one and one-half times the amount of data currently on your hard disk (remember, you saw how to check that in Chapter 1).

Another great thing about external hard drives is that you can start up your Mac from them. So if you have a catastrophic disk failure, and you have a recent duplicate backup, you can restart from the external drive and be up and running again in just a few minutes.

For backup software, you have a choice of many software packages, and I looked at many of them while writing this book. The one I recommend for quick duplicate backups is called SuperDuper!, from Shirt Pocket (www.shirtpocket.com/SuperDuper/).

SuperDuper! costs $19.95, but you can download and use it as a free trial version to perform duplicate backups of your whole hard drive to an external hard drive. If you later want to take advantage of all of the program's features, just pay the registration fee and enter the serial number that Shirt Pocket will e-mail to you.

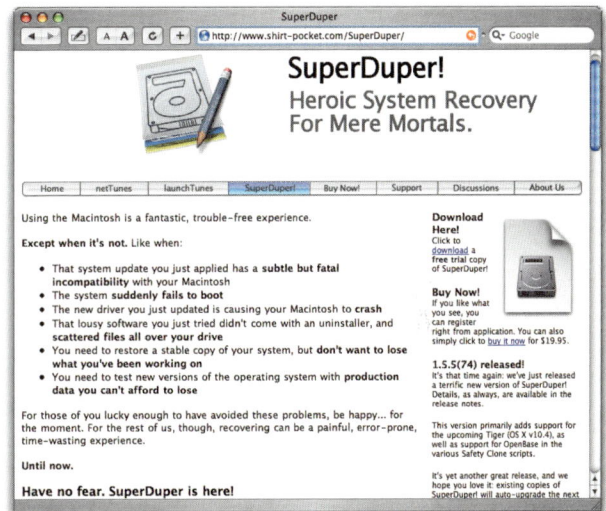

pick files to back up

So what should you back up? You have two choices:

Macintosh HD

Everything, which is what I strongly recommend. That means you will use SuperDuper! or an equivalent program to perform a duplicate backup of your entire hard disk to an external hard disk. The duplicate will be bootable, and can be used to start up your system in the event of a catastrophic hard drive failure.

tom

Just your User folder, which will include only the files in your Home directory. This will include the files that you care about the most, including your documents, pictures, and music. This backup will not be bootable. The reason I don't recommend that you backup only your User folder is that it's much harder to recover from a disaster if you only backed up your personal files.

do the backup

I'm making the assumption in this section that you're using SuperDuper! as your backup software. If you're using something else, refer to the instructions that came with that software package.

1 Begin your backup by quitting all of your open applications.

2 Launch SuperDuper!

3 In the SuperDuper! window, choose your hard drive (the source of the copy) from the pop-up menu on the left, and the external hard drive (the destination of the copy) from the pop-up menu on the right.

Source pop-up menu   Destination pop-up menu

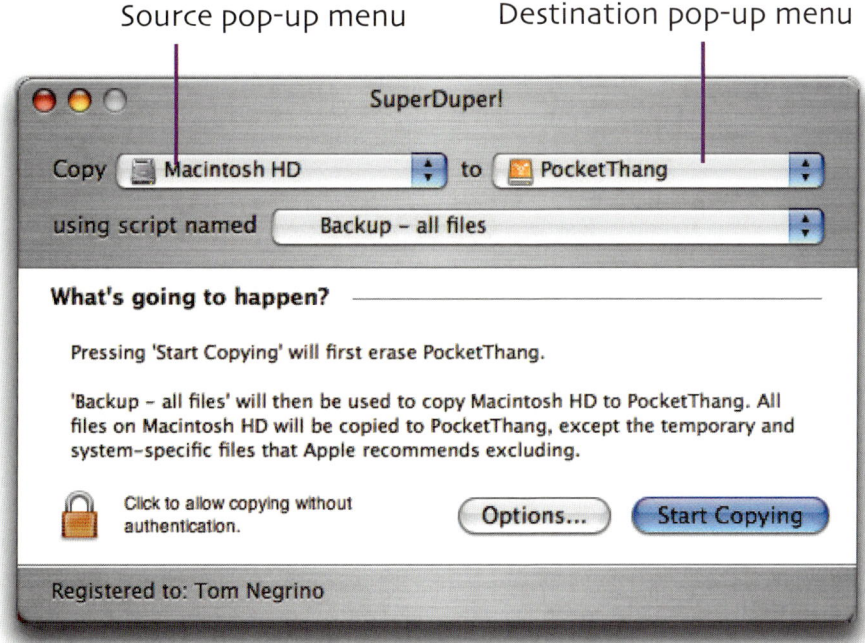

4 In the using script named pop-up menu, choose either Backup – all files or Backup – user files.

do the backup (cont.)

5 Click the Options button. The window changes to show you the backup options.

6 In the Before copy section, check Repair permissions on Macintosh HD. If your hard drive is named something else, you'll see that name in this option instead.

The other Options items are only available in the registered version of SuperDuper!

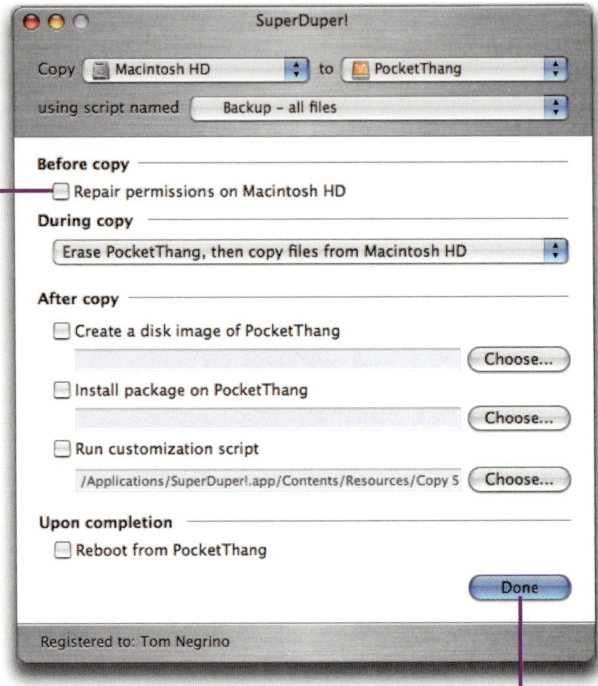

7 Click Done to return to the SuperDuper! window.

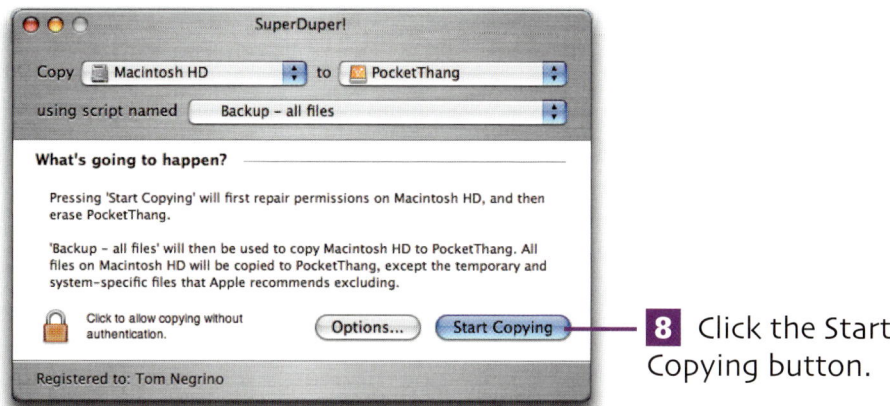

8 Click the Start Copying button.

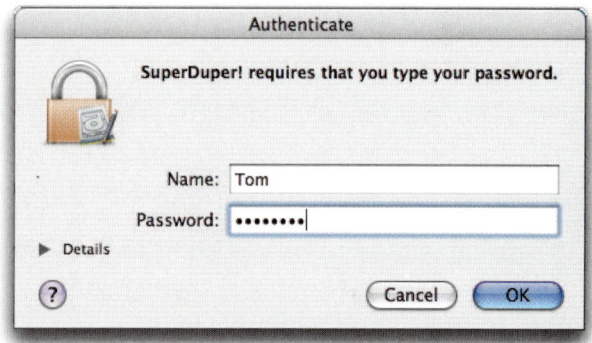

Because the duplication process will erase the external hard drive, you're asked for your password.

Copying all the files on your hard disk will take some time, depending on how much you have to copy and the performance of your external drive. SuperDuper! will keep you informed with progress indicators, and will tell you when the duplicate is complete.

test your backup

If you created a duplicate (and I hope you did), you should test it to make sure that it works to boot your machine. You'll do that by rebooting from the external drive.

1 Choose Apple > System Preferences, then click the Startup Disk icon.

2 Click the icon representing the external hard drive.

3 Click Restart. Your system will restart from the external drive. Once you've verified that the system has booted normally from the external drive, choose Apple > System Preferences > Startup Disk, reset the startup disk to the hard drive inside your computer, and restart again.

extra bits

choose backup tools p. 16

- The reason I don't even suggest backing up to recordable CDs is that at 650 MB, their capacity is just too small for today's hard disks.

- When it comes to the subject of backing up your Mac, I've only scratched the surface in this chapter. If you need more information about backup options and strategies, I recommend that you purchase and download the excellent ebook, Take Control of Mac OS X Backups, by Joe Kissell. It's only $10, and it covers backing up a single computer or a whole network. You can find it at www.takecontrolbooks.com.

- There are two main types of backup: the archive backup, and the duplicate backup. An archive backup contains multiple copies of your files, taken at different times. So you can go into an archive backup set and find a version of a particular file from yesterday or from last month (assuming that you did backups at those two times). Archive backups usually contain just the data files that you create, like your Documents folder, or your User. A duplicate backup makes a complete copy of all or part of your hard disk. In this chapter, I'm just discussing how to do duplicate backups.

- If you get a great deal on a large external backup drive, you can use the same drive to do both duplicate and archive backups. You'll need to partition the drive, which splits one drive into two or more volumes, which show up on your Mac's desktop as though they are different hard drives. For example, I have approximately 65 GB used on my Mac's 160 GB hard drive, and I use an external 160 GB hard drive as my backup device. I partitioned the drive into a 90 GB volume, which I use for my duplicate backup, and a 70 GB volume, which is my archive backup. There is extra space on both volumes to accommodate future growth. You can use Disk Utility, found in /Applications/Utilities/, to partition hard drives into volumes, but because the partitioning process erases the volumes, you'll want to partition your drives before you do any backups.

extra bits

do the backup p. 19

- If you purchase a registration for SuperDuper!, you get access to its Smart Update feature, which allows the program to only copy or delete those files that have changed since the last duplicate. It saves a lot of time compared to the time it takes to do the first duplicate.

3. upgrade to tiger

Now that you've prepared and backed up your computer, it's finally time to upgrade to Tiger. In this chapter, you'll learn about the different upgrade methods, choose the method that works best for you, and install Tiger on your Macintosh.

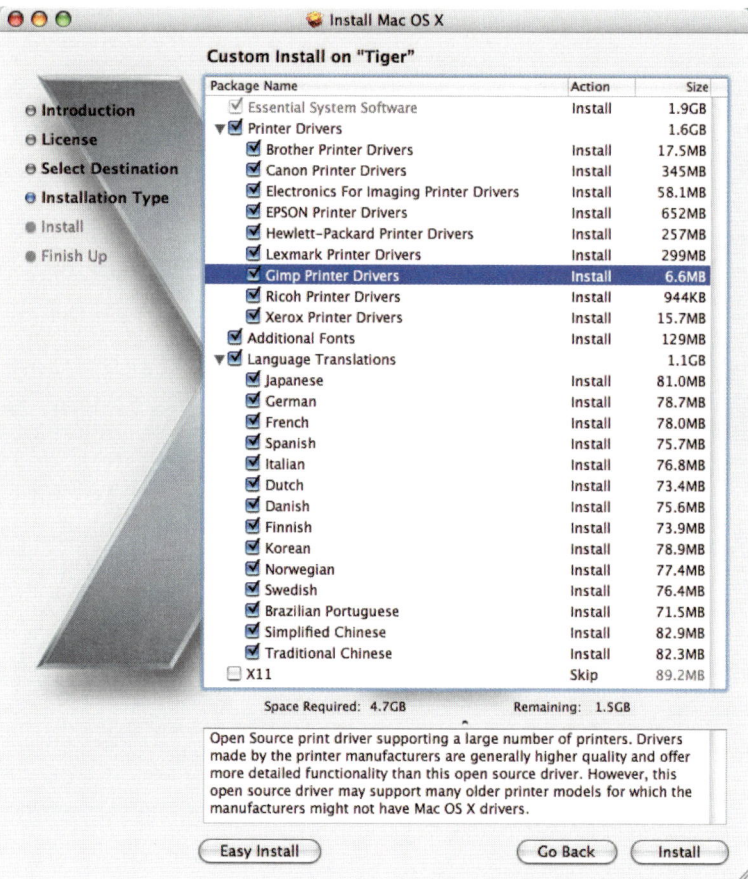

begin the upgrade

If you are installing on a laptop, be sure to plug in its power adapter before you start. The upgrade can take as long as an hour, and you don't want to run out of battery power in the middle of it.

On all Macs, begin by quitting all open programs. Look in the Dock to see which programs are open, switch to each one, and quit the program.

Take the Tiger DVD (or if you got the set of replacement CDs, the first installation CD) and put it into your Mac. The disc appears on the desktop, and a window opens, showing you the Install Mac OS X icon.

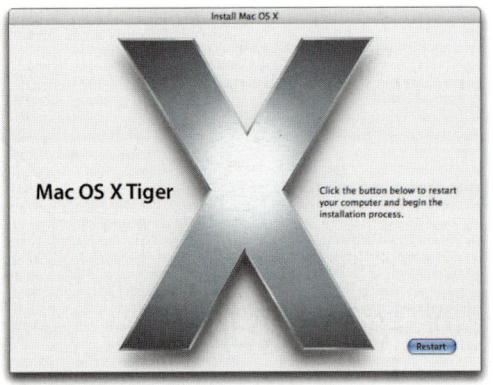

Double-click the icon, and the installer's splash screen appears.

Click the Restart button. The Authenticate screen will appear, asking you to enter your password to continue.

Enter your password and click OK. Your Mac will restart from the DVD or CD.

When the machine restarts, you'll see a dialog that asks you to choose from the many languages the Installer supports. Choose your language, and click the right-pointing arrow button. The Welcome to the Mac OS X Installer screen appears.

check your hard disk

There's one last check that you'll do before you actually install Tiger. It's possible, though unlikely, that there could be damage to the disk directory that might cause the installation to go awry. We'll eliminate that potential problem by using the Disk Utility program to check for directory damage, and repair it if needed.

In the Installer, choose Utilities > Disk Utility. The Disk Utility Program starts up.

Volume list   Message area

In the Volume list, click to select the disk on which you will be installing Tiger. Then click the Repair Disk button.

The message area fills up with information about the progress of the disk repair. If the disk is fine, the last message will be "No repairs were necessary." If a repair was necessary, you'll get a message to that effect.

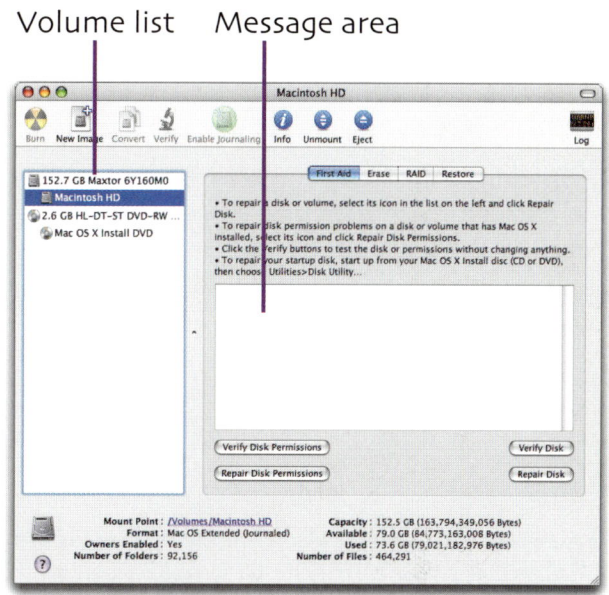

When the repair process is done, choose Disk Utility > Quit Disk Utility. You will return to the Welcome to the Mac OS X Installer screen.

choose upgrade type

On the Welcome to the Mac OS X Installer screen, click Continue. The Software License Agreement screen appears. If you like reading such things, read the license agreement now. Most of us will immediately click Continue. A dialog appears that demands that you agree with the license. Click Agree. The Select a Destination screen appears.

Macintosh HD
152GB (79.2GB Free)

Click the icon of the hard drive where you want to install Tiger.

Now you need to make the most important decision of the upgrade process—what type of upgrade you'll be doing. There are three types of upgrades:

- Upgrade Mac OS X is the default choice. This upgrade is the easiest. The Installer replaces software from your previous version of Mac OS X with the new versions from Tiger, and adds Tiger's new goodies. All of your applications, data files, and user preferences are left in place. The possible drawback is that in rare cases, your Mac won't work properly after the upgrade, due to incompatible login items or disk directory damage that wasn't caught by running Disk Utility.

- Archive and Install installs a fresh copy of Tiger onto your hard drive, and makes a copy of your old system files so that you can manually copy any files you may need after Tiger is working properly. It has an option, Preserve Users and Network Settings, which leaves your user folders unchanged, so all of your documents and preferences are in place and ready to be used as soon as the upgrade is complete.

- Erase and Install completely erases your hard disk, then installs a new copy of Tiger. All of your documents and settings will be wiped away, and you will have to restore them from your backup. The benefit of this kind of upgrade is that you're guaranteed to get a completely operational system when the installation is done.

Which upgrade will be best for you? In the majority of cases, the Upg.
choice will work well, and it is also the fastest. It is also the one that I recommend, as long as you have a bootable backup of your current hard drive, as
discussed in Chapter 2 (and you did do that, right?). If you happen to be one
of the unlucky few who have serious problems with your system after the
upgrade, you can revert back to your previous system with little trouble,
then do an Archive and Install or an Erase and Install upgrade.

Click the Options button at the
bottom of the Installer window. The Install Types dialog
appears.

Choose the radio button next
to the install type that you
want. If you choose Archive
and Install, I recommend that
you also check Preserve Users
and Network Settings. Then
click OK to return to the
Select a Destination screen.
Click Continue.

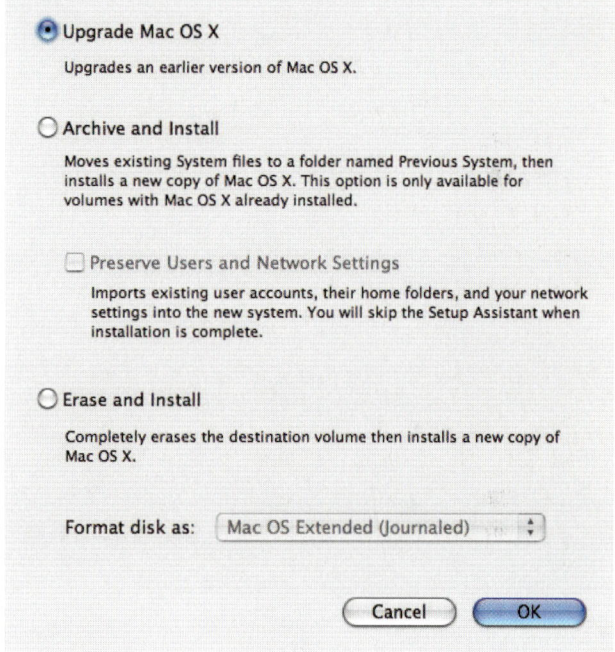

The Easy Install screen appears. You could just click the Upgrade button (or if you chose the Archive and Install or Erase and Install methods, the Install button), but if you do, you'll end up installing many files that you will most likely never use, and that will eat up a significant amount of disk space. So I recommend that you do a customized installation. Click the Customize button at the bottom of the Installer window. The Custom Install screen appears.

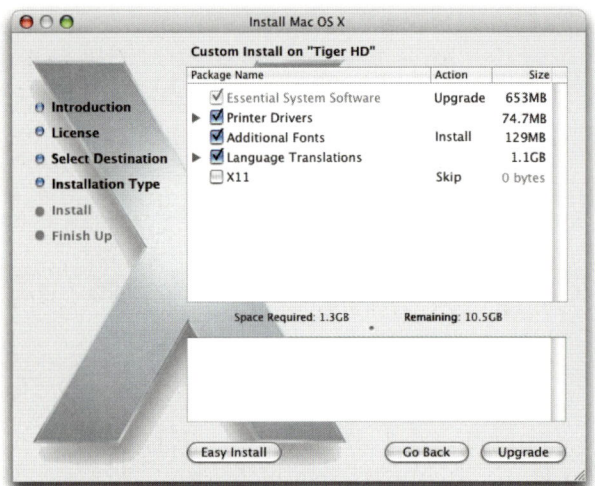

Your mission here is to only install the software that you need. Click the disclosure triangle next to Printer Drivers. The item expands to show you the options.

If you don't own hardware from a particular printer manufacturer, clear the checkbox next to it. The exception is the Gimp Printer Drivers; those are open-source drivers that cover many printers (including older printers that never got updated

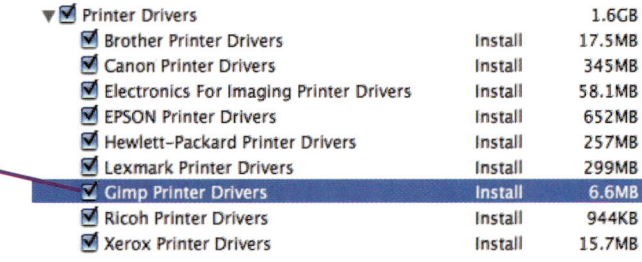

drivers for Mac OS X from their manufacturers), and they're useful to have available. For example, I own an Epson color inkjet printer and a Brother laser printer, so I left those checked, plus the Gimp drivers. The rest I unchecked, saving myself almost a gigabyte of disk space.

The Additional Fonts choice installs fonts for twelve languages listed in the Extra Bits. If you don't need these languages, uncheck the box next to the choice.

▼ ☑ Language Translations		1.1GB
☑ Japanese	Install	81.0MB
☑ German	Install	78.7MB
☑ French	Install	78.0MB
☑ Spanish	Install	75.7MB
☑ Italian	Install	76.8MB
☑ Dutch	Install	73.4MB
☑ Danish	Install	75.6MB
☑ Finnish	Install	73.9MB
☑ Korean	Install	78.9MB
☑ Norwegian	Install	77.4MB
☑ Swedish	Install	76.4MB
☑ Brazilian Portuguese	Install	71.5MB
☑ Simplified Chinese	Install	82.9MB
☑ Traditional Chinese	Install	82.3MB

The Language Translations choice installs translations for the operating system for the languages shown. If you don't intend to operate your Mac in multiple languages, then you don't need these translations, so uncheck the Language Translations box, and all of the indented choices will be cleared. Eliminating languages that you don't use will save another 1.1GB of disk space. If your machine already had the languages installed from a previous installation of Mac OS X, you won't be able to eliminate them.

The X11 choice lets you run applications for the X Window System, which is a standard for graphical user interfaces on UNIX systems. If you don't run X Windows-based programs, there's no need to install X11.

Click Upgrade (or Install, depending on the installation type you chose). The upgrade proceeds. It's time for a break, because the upgrade will take between 20 minutes to an hour, depending on what version of Mac OS X you are upgrading from and the speed of your Mac. The Installer will keep you informed on its progress with an estimated time remaining.

When the upgrade is complete, your Mac will automatically reboot and the Setup Assistant will run. If you chose an Upgrade Mac OS X or Archive and Install (with Preserve Users and Network Settings selected) installation, the Setup Assistant will set up your .Mac account, if you have one, and will send registration information to Apple.

If you chose an Erase and Install installation (or an Archive and Install with Preserve Users and Network Settings turned off), the Setup Assistant will offer to copy your important information from your external FireWire hard drive (or even another Mac). I recommend that you use this "data migration" feature, rather than try to copy items manually. It will also allow you to select your preferred country and keyboard layout; set up your .Mac account (if you have one); set up an initial user account; and send registration information to Apple.

run software update

One of the things that usually happens automatically after you reboot under Tiger for the first time is that the Software Update program should run. You want it to check for updated versions of any Apple software you have installed. Apple often produces updates to their programs or to the operating system itself to address any incompatibilities or problems that became apparent after the initial release. With Tiger, these operating system upgrades will be numbered 10.4.x, where x is an update number. Apple has also taken to releasing monthly security updates, to make sure that Mac OS X maintains its superior reputation for security. I strongly recommend that you install any operating system upgrades or security updates that appear in Software Update.

If Software Update doesn't run automatically, you should run it manually before you get to work using Tiger. Choose Apple > Software Update. The Software Update window appears.

Click in the Install column to select or deselect updates. Click on a particular update to see a description of that update in the lower pane of the window. When you have made your selections, click the Install Items button to download the updates and install them. Depending on the updates you have selected, your machine may need to automatically restart in order to use the new software.

The number in this button will vary, depending on the number of updates you are installing.

upgrade to tiger

extra bits

check your hard disk p. 27

- In Disk Utility, you could click Verify Disk, but then it would check the hard disk, and tell you that there was a problem (if one exists), after which you would just have to click Repair Disk anyway, so you may as well cut to the chase.

- In rare cases, Disk Utility will find disk directory damage that it can't repair. In that case, I suggest that you suspend upgrading to Tiger and do two things. First, you should purchase Disk Warrior, from Alsoft (www.alsoft.com). Disk Warrior is an extra-strength utility that can rebuild a damaged disk directory. Run Disk Warrior on the damaged drive, then make another backup, then continue upgrading to Tiger. Alternatively, you could simply do an Erase and Install installation of Tiger, and allow the Setup Assistant to copy your files back to your Mac's hard drive from your backup drive. When the Installer erases the internal drive it also clears the directory damage (along with everything else on your disk).

choose upgrade type p. 28

- If you have problems with an Upgrade installation and you need to revert to your old system from your backup, I recommend that you next try an Archive and Install upgrade, then if you still have trouble, an Erase and Install installation.

- If you choose to do an Erase and Install installation, after your computer reboots into Tiger the Setup Assistant will run and offer to copy all of your personal files from another volume. If you made a backup onto another hard drive, the Setup Assistant will do most of the work of copying your files back to your main drive for you.

- Erase and Install gives you a choice of how you want to format your hard drive. Your choices are Mac OS Extended (Journaled), which is the one you should choose, or UNIX File System, which is for very specialized installations.

extra bits

pick upgrade options p. 30

- The Additional Fonts choice installs fonts for Chinese, Korean, Arabic, Hebrew, Thai, Cyrillic, Devangari, Gujarati, Punjabi, Armenian, Cherokee, and Inuktitut.

- If you can't eliminate foreign-language fonts during the installation (because they are already present from a previous installation), you can at least turn them off so that they don't appear in applications. Open the Font Book program (it's in your Applications folder). Choose All Fonts in the Collection column, then look for foreign fonts in the Font column. Click on a font family in the Font column to select it and get a preview of the font. If it's a font you want to turn off, choose Edit > Disable fontname Family (where fontname is the selected font). Then quit Font Book.

- It can make sense to install all of the different printer driver options if you are installing on a laptop, and you want maximum flexibility in printing to any printers you might encounter while you are on the road.

- If you don't install a particular bit of software during your initial Tiger install (for example, if you purchase a printer from a different manufacturer), you can still install it later. Insert your Tiger installation disk, and double-click the Optional Installs icon. The Installer will start up, and you can choose to install applications, additional fonts, language translations, or printer drivers.

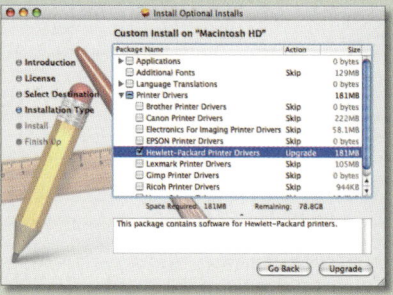

run software update p. 32

- Software Update sometimes offers an update that you can't use. This is usually new software for Apple hardware such as an iPod, iSight, or AirPort wireless router. If you don't own the hardware, there's no reason to install the software. You can keep the update from appearing in the Software Update list by selecting the update and choosing Update > Ignore Update.

4. set up tiger

Once your machine restarts into Tiger, you'll have the opportunity—and perhaps the need—to reinstall some software and set up your Mac so that you and your family can work better and more efficiently. In this chapter, you'll learn what to do right after the upgrade; how to reinstall software and printers; and how to set up your Mac so that different users of the same machine can keep out of each other's hair.

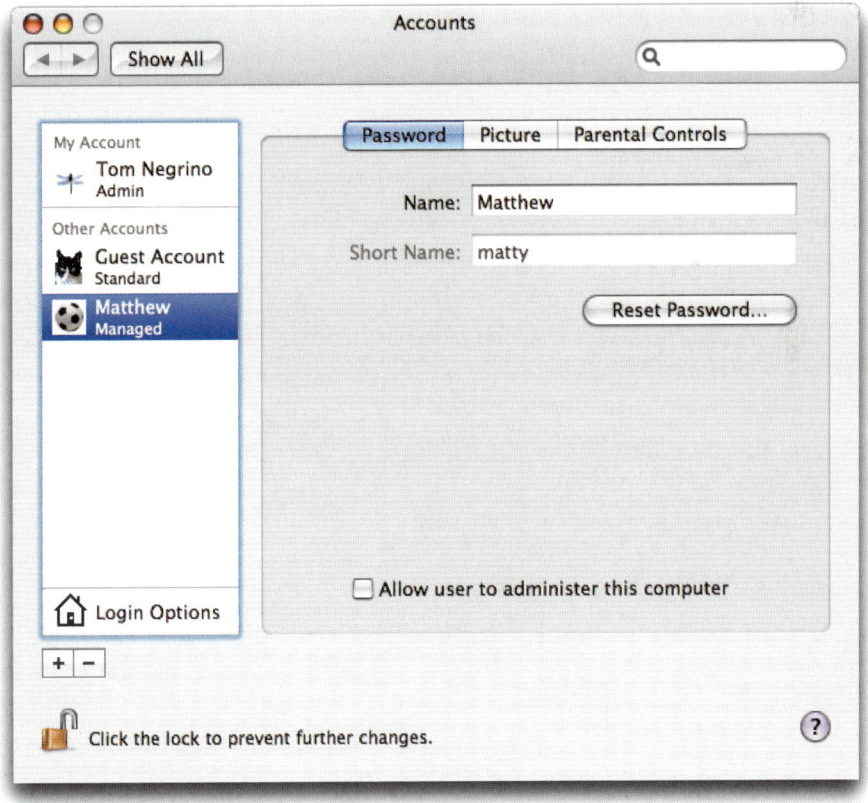

don't panic

Immediately after you boot into Tiger for the first time, you will notice that your Mac seems to be running a bit slowly, and you may be able to hear a lot of hard disk access. It's not a problem, it's a new Tiger feature at work. Spotlight, the new integrated search technology, needs to index all of your attached hard drives, and it does so automatically. You can't stop it, so relax. Indexing your drives can take a few minutes to a couple of hours or so, depending on how many files you have. While the index is being built, you'll see the Spotlight icon in the upper-right corner of the screen pulsing, and you won't be able to use Spotlight (if you try, you'll see an estimate of how much time is remaining to complete the index).

Spotlight icon

After the initial indexing is complete, you should never have to wait for indexing again; Spotlight silently indexes files as soon as you create or modify them. You'll learn about using Spotlight in Chapter 7.

After Spotlight finishes indexing, you'll notice something else about Tiger: it's faster than Panther or Jaguar. On the same hardware, you'll see that windows resize faster; scrolling happens a bit quicker; and applications launch more rapidly. Interestingly, you'll probably experience more improvement with slower hardware (because Panther was already pretty snappy on fast hardware). My desktop machine is a Dual 2.5 GHz G5 Power Mac, and upgrading to Tiger was a definite improvement. But I really noticed the difference on my 12" PowerBook, which has only an 867 MHz G4 processor.

reinstall software

This is the point at which you may need to reinstall software, especially driver software for input devices such as mice, trackballs, keyboards, or graphics tablets. If you're using an Apple mouse or keyboard, you don't have to worry, because drivers for those devices are built into Mac OS X. If you did an Upgrade installation, you may not need to do any reinstalling of software drivers at all, though it's not a bad idea to install the latest versions of your driver software anyway.

Third-party drivers may need to be updated, so it's best to check with the manufacturer of your device. Here is a list of the most common manufacturers of input devices. Check on their Web sites to download and install the latest version of the driver software for your device.

- Griffin Technology (USB control devices, USB remote controls, USB and FireWire audio interfaces): www.griffintechnology.com/software/.

- Kensington (mice, trackballs, and keyboards): www.kensington.com.

- Logitech (mice, trackballs, keyboards, Harmony remote controls): www.logitech.com.

- Microsoft (mice and keyboards): www.microsoft.com/hardware/mouseandkeyboard/Download.mspx.

- Wacom (graphics tablets): www.wacom.com/productsupport/.

Printers and scanners may require updated software. Though Tiger includes printer drivers for many printers (lots more than previous versions of OS X), you should check for updates. Also check the Web site of your scanner's manufacturer (if you have one, of course).

reinstall software (cont.)

If you use any utility software, you should check the manufacturers' Web sites to make sure that you're running the latest updates. If not, download and install the current versions. If you're not sure which version you have installed, you can find the application in the Finder, then choose File > Get Info. The version number is shown in the resulting window.

Version number ————

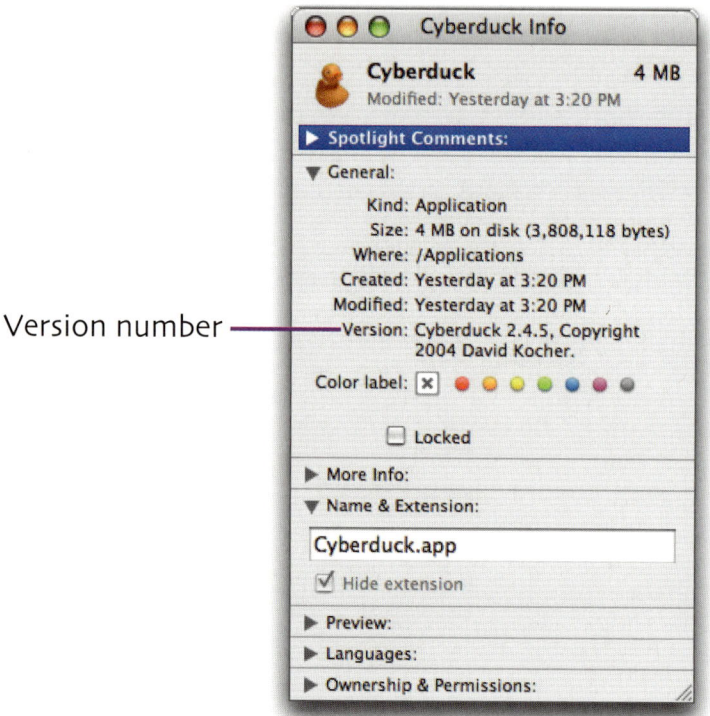

Many application packages were updated after Tiger's release, either to fix bugs and incompatibilities, or to take advantage of Tiger's new abilities. You can either check each manufacturer's site, or you can take a look at two pages that track updates. Macworld magazine's Tiger software update summary is at www.macworld.com/2005/05/news/tigerupdates/, and Macintouch's Third-Party Updates page is at www.macintouch.com/tigercompat.html. If you find software that you own on one of these pages, download and install the update from the manufacturer's site.

set up printers

If you used the Upgrade Mac OS X installation option, chances are you'll find that your printers are still listed in the Print dialog, so you should be able to print normally. But for some mysterious reason, you may find that after the upgrade you can't print, so you will need to set up your printer again. If you used the Archive and Install or Erase and Install upgrade methods, you will have to go through printer setup. The setup process differs, depending on whether your Mac is directly connected to the printer via a USB cable, or if you are part of a network and are setting up a printer that is also attached to the network.

To set up a USB printer, follow these steps:

1 Make sure that your printer is plugged into your Mac and that the printer is turned on.

2 Open the Printer Setup Utility, which is in /Applications/ Utilities/.

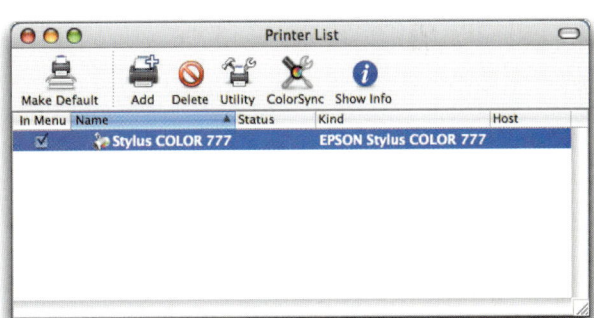

3 In most cases, Mac OS X will detect a printer attached via USB and automatically add it to the Printer List. If your printer shows up, you're done, and you can quit the Printer Setup Utility.

4 If your printer does not show up, you should go through the troubleshooting steps listed in the Printer Setup Utility Help. Choose Help > Printer Setup Utility Help.

set up printers (cont.)

If you are setting up a printer networked via AppleTalk, follow these steps:

1 Open the Printer Setup Utility, which is in /Applications/Utilities/.

2 In the Printer List, click Add.

3 The Printer Browser appears. After a moment, your printer should appear. When it does, select it in the list. Mac OS X will query the printer and select the appropriate printer driver.

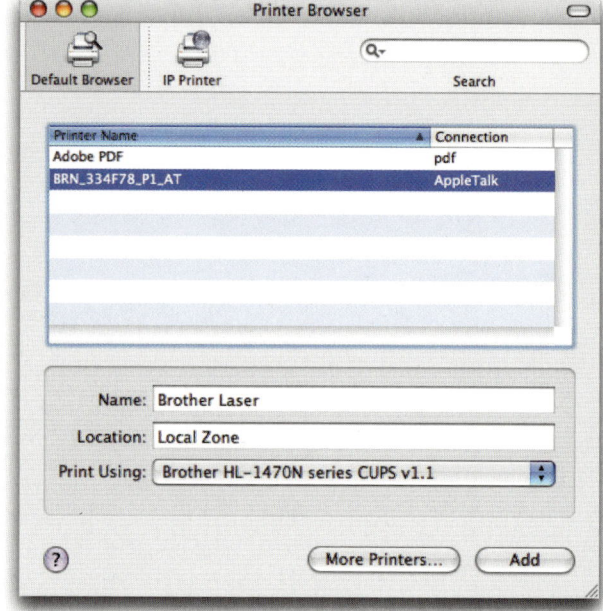

4 If you want, change the name of the printer in the Name field. For example, my Brother laser printer showed up with the name BRN_334F78_P1_AT, which isn't exactly a friendly name. I changed it to Brother Laser.

5 Click the Add button, which closes the Printer Browser and adds the printer to the Printer List.

set up tiger

If you're setting up a printer networked via TCP/IP, follow these steps. You'll need to know the IP address of the printer.

1 Open the Printer Setup Utility, and click Add in the Printer List.

2 In the Printer Browser, click IP Printer.

3 In the Protocol pop-up menu, choose the printing protocol specified in the printer's documentation. It will probably be Line Printer Daemon – LPD, so try that one first.

4 In the Address field, enter the IP address of the printer and press the Tab key. Mac OS X will query the printer and select the appropriate printer driver.

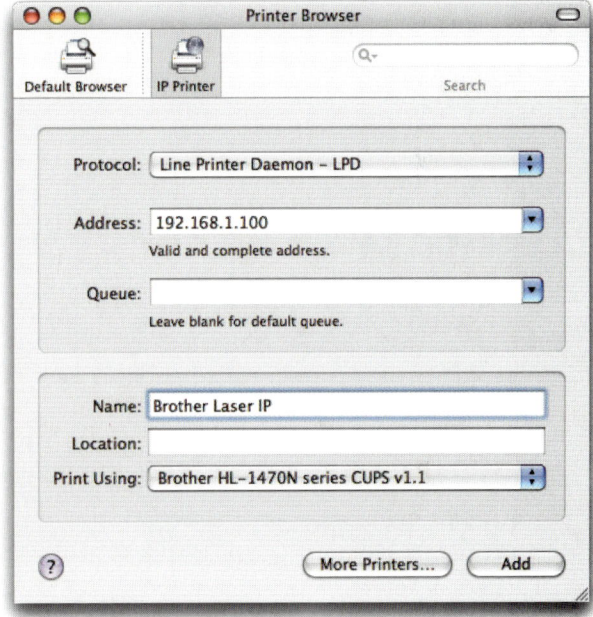

5 If you want, change the name of the printer in the Name field.

6 Click the Add button, which closes the Printer Browser and adds the printer to the Printer List.

set up multiple users

One of the great things about Mac OS X is that it is a multi-user system. That means that if you have more than one person using a particular machine, each person can have his or her own user account. Each account is separated from the others, so documents, folders, and preferences from each person can be kept entirely separate. When you set up a Mac OS X account, you are assigned a home folder, which has your name and the house icon.

Files and folders in your home folder belong to you; if there are any other users on the machine, they can't access files or folders in your home folder.

What a user can do in Mac OS X is dependent on their user permissions. Permissions tell your Mac who owns a file or folder, and what rights the owner has (to read or write a file, or launch an application).

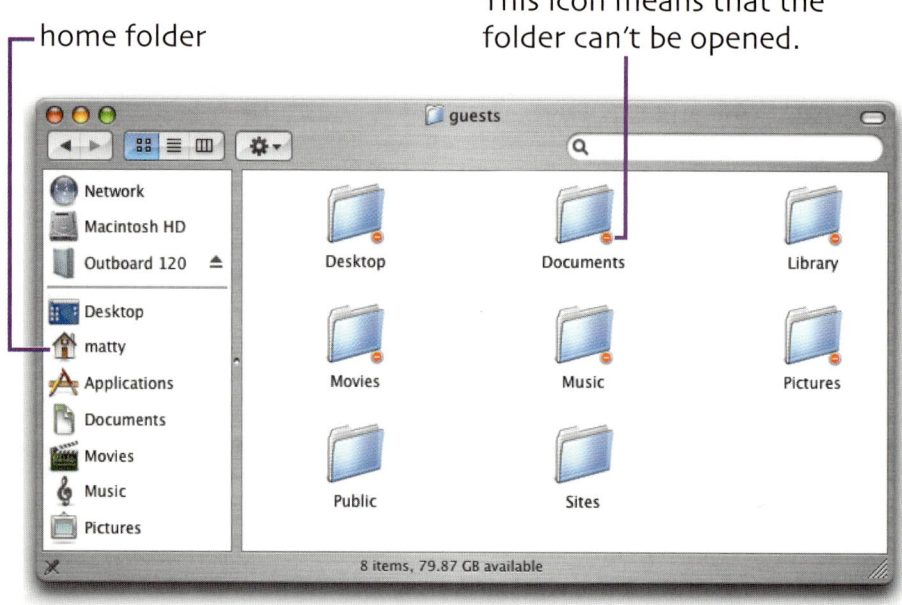

home folder

This icon means that the folder can't be opened.

When you install Mac OS X, a single user account is created, and it is an administrator account. Without going into too much detail, an administrator has permissions to do almost anything on the system, including create and delete other accounts; change permissions on files and folders; install software on the system for use by all users; and modify or delete any file or folder.

There are two other kinds of Mac OS X accounts, standard and managed accounts. A managed account is the perfect account type for children, and we'll talk about this type in the next section. A standard account is useful to set up for users other than you. Standard account owners can access files and folders in their own home folders; have their own preferences; and install software for their own use. Here's an example of how I use standard accounts on my Macs. I often travel with my PowerBook, and sometimes my wife travels with me and uses my laptop. We prefer different setups for our Macs; for example, I like the Dock hidden and on the right side of the screen. She likes it on the left side of the screen, always visible. I created a standard account on my PowerBook for her, and when she uses the machine, she simply logs into her account, and all of her preferences are there, along with documents and folders she's created. Mac OS X makes it easy to change users with a feature called fast user switching, discussed later in this chapter.

Similarly, if your family shares a single computer, setting up separate accounts for each family member gives them each their own private home folder for their documents, photos, music, movies, and so forth. I also like to set up a standard account for guests who may need to use the computer.

set up multiple users (cont.)

To set up additional standard accounts on your Mac, follow these steps:

1 Choose Apple > System Preferences, then click the Accounts icon.

2 Click the Lock button. The Authenticate dialog appears. Enter your user name and password, and then click OK.

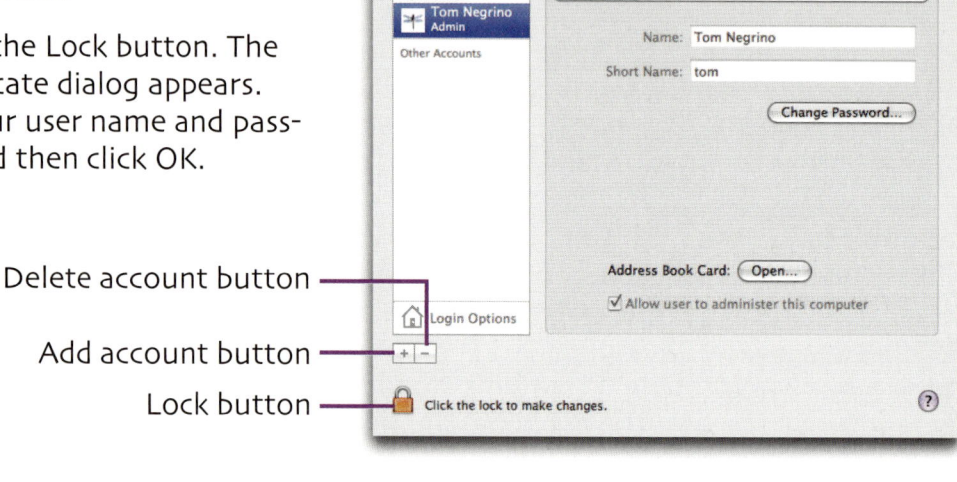

Delete account button

Add account button

Lock button

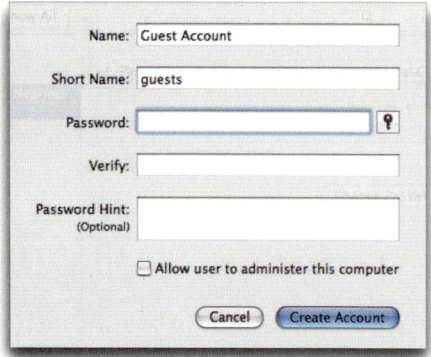

3 Click the Add account button. The account information dialog appears. The Name field is for the user's full or long name. Fill out the Name, then press the Tab key. After you press Tab, you will see that Mac OS X automatically fills in the Short Name field in lowercase without spaces. The Short Name is used for the name of the user's home folder, and it doesn't have to be the same as the long name. You can shorten it as needed. For example, on my Mac the long name is Tom Negrino, but my short name is tom.

4 If you want, change the short name from the suggested one that was filled in for you. You can't easily change the short name once the account is created, so make sure that it's the one you want now.

5 Enter a password, then enter it again in the Verify field. If you aren't worried about security for this account, you can leave the password fields empty. Click Create Account. If you didn't enter passwords, Tiger warns you that this is insecure. Click OK.

6 After a moment, the new account appears in the Accounts window.

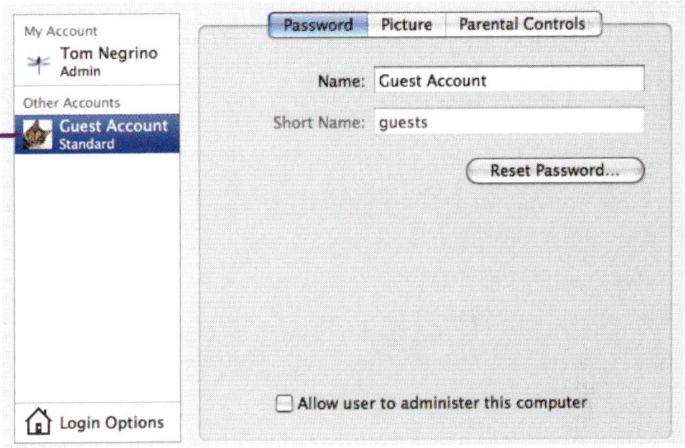

Picture well

7 All user accounts have a picture associated with them, to make it easy to distinguish between accounts at a glance. To assign a picture to the account you just created, click the Picture tab, then drag a picture from the Apple Pictures, or drag an image file from the desktop into the picture well.

set parental controls

A managed account sets parental controls, which limit the things a user can do with an account. You can limit the following:

- Mail: only allow the Mail user to exchange emails with a specified list of correspondents.

- Finder & System: prevent the user from opening System Preferences, modifying the Dock, or burning CDs and DVDs; or use only specified applications.

- iChat: only allow the user to chat with a specified list of buddies.

- Safari: only allow access to specified Web sites.

- Dictionary: prevent access to certain words, such as profanity.

As you can see, these sorts of controls are a real help to parents who want to shield their kids from objectionable material or make sure that they can only use certain applications.

To enable parental controls, make sure you are logged into an administrator account, then open the Accounts pane of System Preferences. Select a standard account in the window, then click the Parental Controls tab.

Click the checkboxes next to the categories that you want to limit. For each category, click the Configure button. Each one is different, but is fairly self-explanatory. For example, the Finder & System controls make it easy to identify which applications you want to allow.

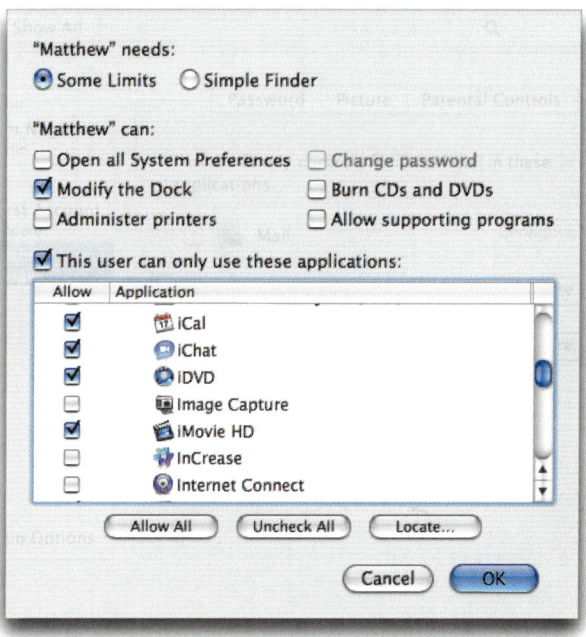

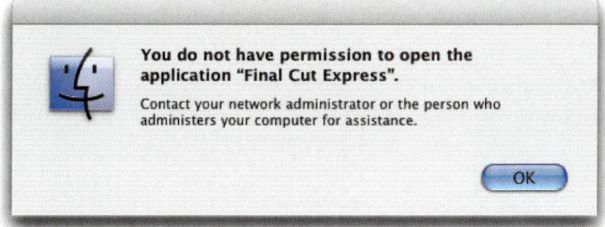

If the user tries to open an application that they are not authorized to use, the system lets them know.

switch between users

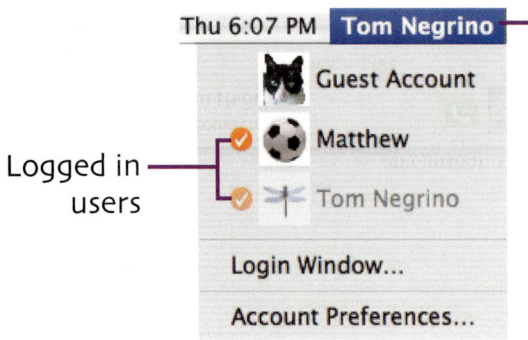

Logged in users

In order to easily change users, you'll need to turn on fast user switching. This puts a new menu in the upper-right corner of your screen, the User menu.

To enable fast user switching, open the Accounts pane of System Preferences. Click the Login Options button.

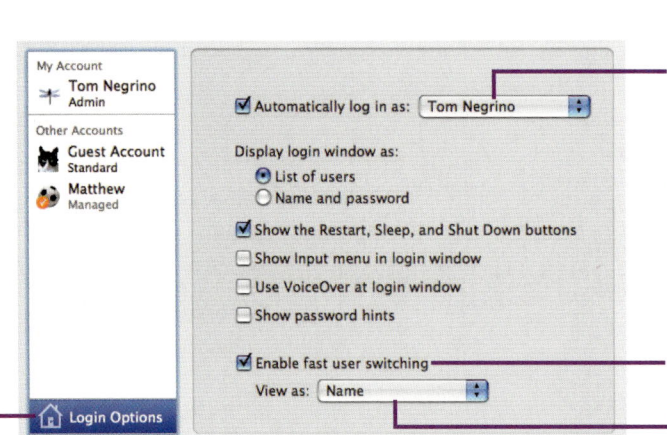

You can set your machine to automatically log in you or any other user by choosing the user from the pop-up menu.

To turn on fast user switching, click Enable fast user switching.

You can choose how users are identified in the User menu: by Name, Short name, or Icon.

Close the System Preferences window to save your changes.

To switch users, choose a user name from the User menu. If the user has a password, the Login window will appear, and you'll be prompted to enter the password.

extra bits

reinstall software p. 37

- There are a few programs that aren't included with Tiger, though they came with previous versions of Mac OS X. Microsoft's Internet Explorer Web browser is gone, and so is Allume's StuffIt Expander. If you already had these programs on your machine before the upgrade, they haven't gone anywhere; they just don't come with Tiger. Internet Explorer was superseded by Apple's own Safari, of course, and Explorer hasn't been updated in a few years anyway, nor will it be updated in the future on the Macintosh, according to Microsoft. If you have a need to uncompress archives in the StuffIt format (they have the file extension .sit or .sitx) and you don't have StuffIt Expander, you can download a copy for free at www.stuffit.com/mac/. You can compress and archive files and folder using the Finder's built-in ability; just select what you want to archive in the Finder, and choose File > Create Archive.

- Don't be surprised that you have to update software after a major system upgrade. It's a normal part of the process. After I upgraded to Tiger, I ended up downloading and reinstalling approximately 20 different programs.

- There may be additional settings you need to turn on after your upgrade. For example, I found that the upgrade turned off fax receipt. If you receive faxes on your computer, you can turn it back on by choosing Apple > System Preferences, then clicking the Print & Fax icon. Click the Faxing tab, then click the checkbox next to Receive faxes on this computer. I also find that in the Save to pop-up menu, it is better to pick the Faxes folder, as opposed to the Shared Faxes folder. If you use the latter folder, you must enter an administrator's password whenever you want to trash a fax from the Shared Faxes folder. It's a pain.

- When you first use an updated application that requires a password, you'll get an alert that lets you know that the application wants to access your keychain (which is what Mac OS X calls the encrypted file that stores your passwords). This is good from a security standpoint, but you don't need to see this alert more than once per updated application. Click the Change All button to tell your keychain that it's OK to use the updated application.

extra bits

set up printers p. 39

- Apple's AirPort Extreme Base Station and AirPort Express wireless routers have a USB port, to which you can hook up many models of printer. If you connect wirelessly to the router from a laptop or other AirPort-equipped Mac, you can print to the printer. You'll need to set up your Mac to use the printer attached to the wireless router. This should be easy, because the printer should show up in the Printer Browser. See the Printer Setup Utility Help if you have a problem connecting to a wireless shared printer.

- Bonjour is the new name in Tiger for Rendezvous, Apple's zero-configuration networking protocol (thank a legal dispute for the name change). Bonjour allows network devices to find and connect to each other with no user configuration required. Some network-capable printers are compatible with Bonjour, and they will show up in the Printer Browser. Other Mac OS X programs that use Bonjour are iTunes (to find shared music libraries); iChat (to find other chat users on the network); iPhoto (to find shared photo libraries); and many third-party programs.

set up multiple users p. 42

- You can't choose the long and short names "Guest" and "guest," respectively, for a user account you create. Those names are reserved by the system.

- Sometimes you want to make changes to a user's account, so you try to click on the user in the Accounts pane and can't because it is dimmed. That's because the user is logged in. Switch to that user account, log them off, then go back to the administrator's account and make the changes you want.

- The subject of multiple users is much more involved than I have room for here. For more information, I recommend Take Control of Users & Accounts in Tiger, by Kirk McElhearn. You can purchase this ebook online at www.takecontrolbooks.com/tiger-users.html.

switch between users p. 48

- If you want to shut down or restart the Mac, and you have more than one account in use, you are required to enter an administrator username and password.

- When you switch from one account to another, be sure to save your documents first. An administrator can shut down the Mac by entering an administrator password, but that doesn't save open documents in accounts that aren't active. And if your Mac crashes, documents that are open in the non-active accounts will lose any unsaved changes.

5. customize your system

Now that you're running Tiger, it's time to make it run the way that you want it to. Mac OS X has always been easy to customize, and Tiger gives you even more customization options.

In this chapter, you'll learn how to customize the Desktop, Dock, and Finder windows; manage window clutter; and set keyboard shortcuts for the system or for applications. By the time you're done reading this chapter, you'll have shown Tiger who's the boss and customized your computer so that you get the most out of it. You certainly don't need to do all the customizations that I suggest, but you should make the customizations that match your needs.

setup finder windows

Mac users spend a lot of time in the Finder, so it makes sense to set up the Finder so that it works the way that is best for you, rather than the way that Apple sets the Finder up by default. You can adjust the view of Finder windows to show or display the items that you want, and you can use Finder windows to help you organize your projects and get your work done more efficiently.

For a moment, let's think about the job of the Finder (as well as closely related items, such as Open and Save dialogs). They help you locate your applications and documents, so anything that you can do to make that process easier and faster will save you a little time here and a little time there. In the course of a year, a few seconds' speed improvement whenever you use the Finder or Open and Save dialogs can add up to a lot of productive hours.

You can customize the initial view of a Finder window by changing a new window, then closing it. The Finder will remember your changes from then on. Here's how you make that customization.

1 Switch to the Finder, then close any windows that happen to be open.

2 Choose File > New Finder Window, or press Command-N. A window opens, set to the default settings. You can see that these settings include where the window appears on the desktop; the window's size; that the window's contents are in icon view; a particular set of tools are available in the window's toolbar; and that the sidebar is visible. We'll get to customizing the sidebar and toolbar later in this chapter.

customize your system

3 If you want, change the window's location on the screen by dragging it by its title bar, then resize the window by clicking and dragging its lower-right corner.

4 Set the view by clicking in the view controller. I prefer list view, but you can choose any view you like.

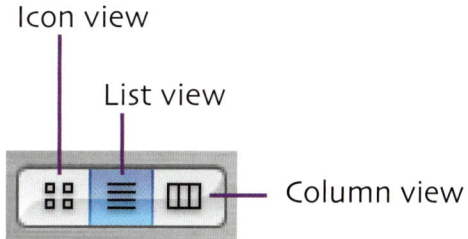

Icon view

List view

Column view

5 Further customize the view you just picked by choosing View > Show View Options. The window that appears is different, depending on which view you chose. I find it most useful to set the icon size and text size.

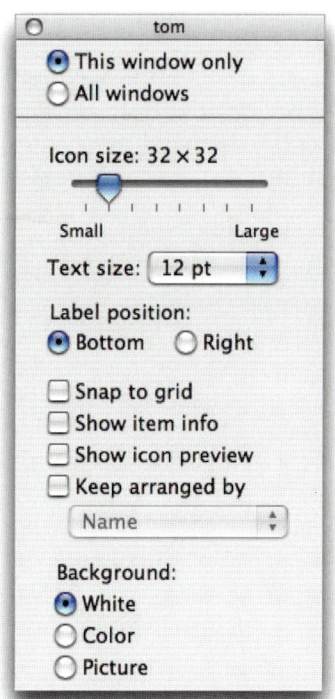

View as Icons options

View as List options

View as Columns options

6 If you choose the icon or list views, you have the choice of This window only or All windows in the View options window. In this case, choose This window only.

7 To save the changes you've made as the default window choice, you must close the window now. After that, whenever you open a new Finder window, it will reflect the choices you just made.

You can also set which folder opens when you choose File > New Finder Window. Choose Finder > Preferences, then click the General tab. From the New Finder windows open pop-up menu, pick the folder you want new Finder windows to show.

customize the sidebar

The sidebar is the area found on the left side of Finder windows, and also in Open and Save dialogs. You can use it to quickly jump to places on your computer that you use frequently, such as folders, volumes, your Applications folder, and more. Clicking on an icon in the sidebar changes the Finder window or the Open or Save dialog to the location represented by the icon. In the Finder, if you drag and drop an icon onto an icon of a folder in the sidebar, it moves or copies the item into that folder.

Apple populates the sidebar with a standard set of locations, but you can customize it quite a bit. Changes that you make in the sidebar in Finder windows are reflected in the sidebar in Open and Save dialogs.

The volumes in the top section of the sidebar are placed there according to the Finder Preferences; we'll discuss those a bit later. The items in the bottom section are your working folders.

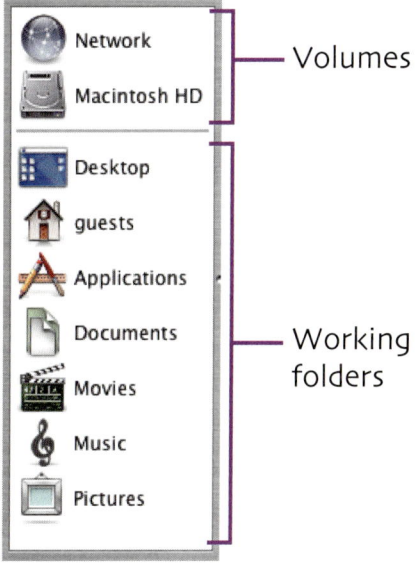

The first thing that you might want to do is get rid of locations that you may not use very often. After all, the whole point of the sidebar is to let you jump to places you want to go; if you don't go to one of the default places on the sidebar, you should make room for places you do want. For example, I don't need to go into my Music or Movies folders very often, so I removed them from my sidebar.

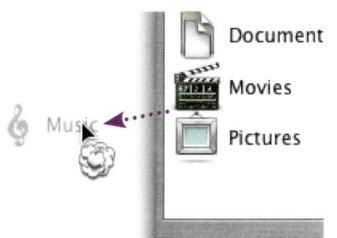

To remove an icon from the sidebar, click on it and drag it out of the window. It disappears in a puff of animated smoke.

customize the sidebar (cont.)

To add a folder to the sidebar, drag it into the sidebar. It's important to drag it in between any icons you already have in the sidebar, or below them (if you drag the folder's icon onto a folder already in the sidebar, it will move the folder you're dragging, as noted above). A blue line shows you where the icon will go when you release the mouse button. For example, I have a folder called Book Projects that I use a lot, so I dragged it into the sidebar.

To change which volume icons appear in the sidebar, choose Finder > Preferences, then click the Sidebar tab. To get rid of items in the sidebar, clear the checkboxes next to those items. For instance, I don't need instant access to the top level of the computer, my iDisk, or the network browser, so I turned those options off, which eliminated those icons from the sidebar.

customize the toolbar

The toolbar is the area found at the top of Finder windows. It provides tools you can use to perform actions such as creating a new folder or changing a window's view. It also has Back and Forward buttons you can use to move through folders you have recently viewed in that window, similar to the way you can move forward and back in a Web browser.

You can customize what you want to have in the toolbar, just like you can with the sidebar. Open a Finder window, then choose View > Customize Toolbar. The customize dialog slides down from the top of the window.

Drag the items you want from the dialog into the toolbar; you can also drag items you don't want off the toolbar while the dialog is open. Use the Show pop-up menu at the bottom of the dialog to display the toolbar items by Icon Only (the default); with icons and a text label; or with text only. Click Done when you are finished customizing. Toolbar customizations affect all Finder windows.

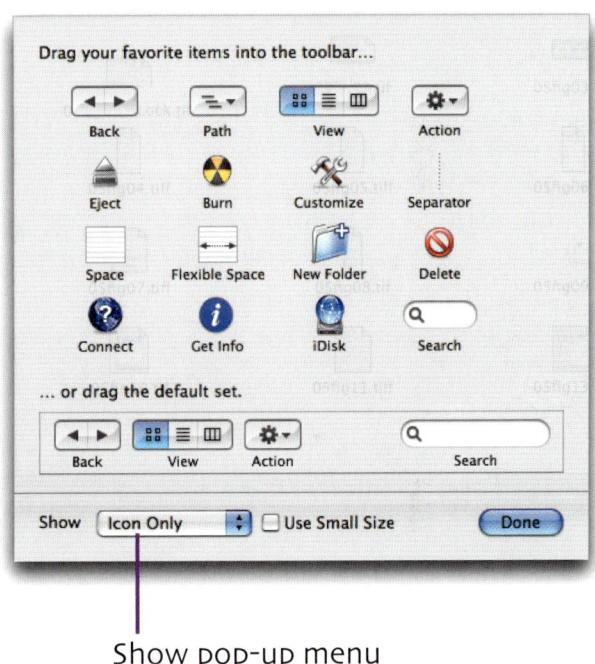

Show pop-up menu

customize the toolbar (cont.)

An especially useful addition to the toolbar is the Path icon, which shows you the path to the folder that you are in, and allows you to easily navigate back up the folder hierarchy.

You can also drag icons of folders or volumes into the toolbar, where they work in much the same way they would if you added them to the sidebar. The difference is that you only see the toolbar in Finder windows, not Open and Save dialogs, so you can put items that you want only in the Finder in the toolbar. For example, I keep the icon of a networked file server in the toolbar, so I can mount it and get to its contents in one step. To put an icon into the toolbar, drag the icon over the toolbar of a Finder window, then wait a moment. After a short pause, a plus sign in a green circle will appear, indicating that you can release the mouse button. When you do release it, the icon appears in the toolbar.

set up your desktop

You can choose what icons you want to appear on your desktop, and you can change the desktop pattern and make other miscellaneous customizations. Choose Finder > Preferences, and click the General tab.

Some people prefer to keep their desktop as uncluttered as possible, and if you are one of those people, you'll want to clear the checkboxes in the choices under Show these items on the Desktop. Having been a Mac user for a very long time, I'm very used to having hard disks, file servers, and removable media appear on the desktop, so I leave these options enabled.

The option Always open folders in a new window is useful for people who don't mind having a blizzard of windows covering their screen. Consider turning on this option; you can always turn it off again if you don't like the results.

You change your desktop pattern in System Preferences. Choose Apple > System Preferences, then click Desktop & Screen Saver, then click the Desktop tab.

Click on one of the categories in the scrolling list on the left, then select one of the pictures in the list on the right to apply it to your desktop. If you have iPhoto installed, scroll down the list on the left, and you can access albums in your iPhoto library.

customize the dock

Like so much of the Mac OS X interface, the Dock can be customized to include icons for applications, folders, and even documents that you use often. To add an icon to the Dock, open the window containing that icon, then drag the icon from the window to the Dock. Items on the Dock move out of the way to make room for the new item. When you release the mouse button, the icon stays in the Dock. Dragging an icon to the Dock does not move it from its original location; rather, it places a copy in the Dock pointing to the original item.

When you drag an item to the Dock, drag applications to the left of (or above, if you keep your Dock on the right or left side of the screen) the divider line, and folders, documents, and servers to the right of (or below) the line.

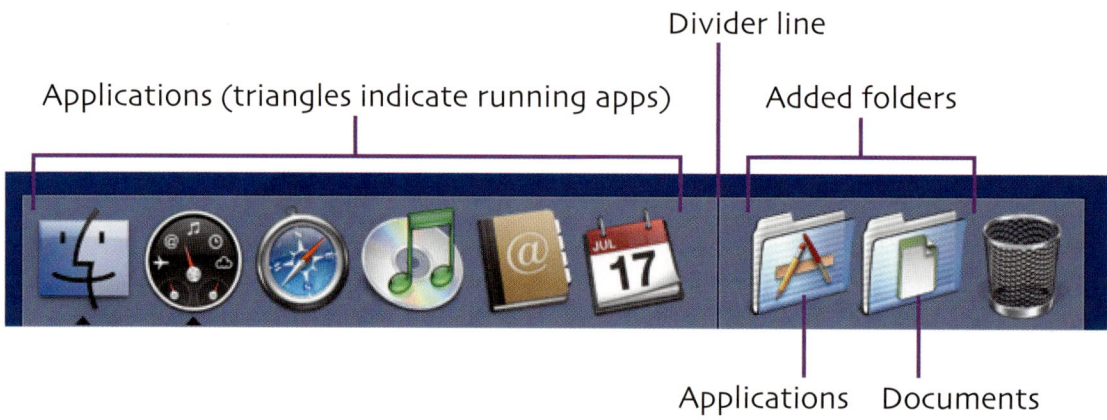

Divider line

Applications (triangles indicate running apps)

Added folders

Applications   Documents

I like to add my Applications folder to the Dock, so that I always have immediate access to all of my applications without having to rummage through a Finder window.

To remove an item from the Dock, simply drag the item from the Dock to the desktop. The item is removed from the Dock in a puff of animated smoke. Removing an icon from the Dock does not delete it from your hard disk.

You can set the basic look and behavior of the Dock by choosing Apple > System Preferences, then clicking the Dock icon.

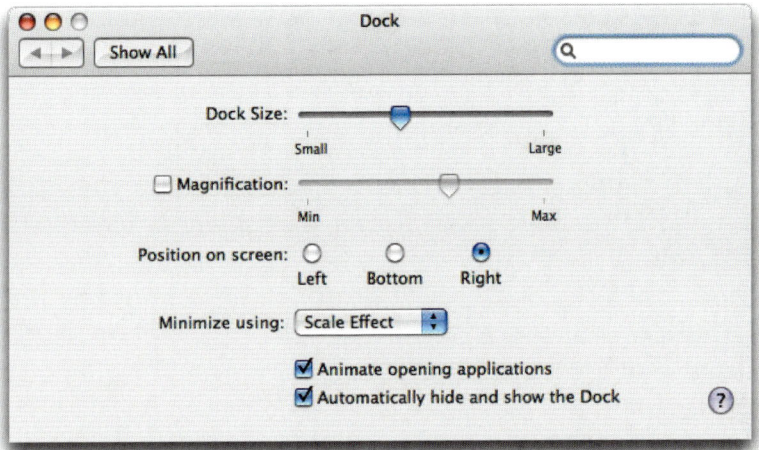

Use the slider to set the Dock size. As you move the slider, you'll see the Dock change in size. If you prefer to keep the Dock at a fairly small size, you might want to use the Magnification setting. Click the checkbox next to Magnification, then use the slider to control how large the icons in the Dock will appear when you move your mouse pointer over them.

Choose the Dock's screen position with the radio buttons: either the left, bottom, or right side of the screen.

Finally, enable Automatically hide and show the Dock to keep the Dock out of the way when you are not using it.

set up exposé

Managing windows is a pain. It's easy (heck, it's practically required) to have multiple applications open under Mac OS X, and each application has at least one, and often many windows. Managing all the windows from even one application can be tricky, because under Mac OS X, when you make an application active, all of its windows do not come to the fore, and some of them can easily be hidden behind windows from the other inactive applications. Many applications have a Bring All to Front command, but not all do.

The Exposé feature makes window management easier by making it easy to see all the open windows in all applications, all the open windows in a single application, or temporarily move application windows off the screen so that you have easy access to the desktop. You can trigger Exposé by pressing shortcut keys or by using one or more of the corners of the screen as a "hot" corner. Moving your mouse pointer into one of the hot corners triggers the Exposé action that you set for that corner.

Press F9 to show all the windows from all applications. Note that the iTunes window is highlighted, because I've moved my mouse over that window.

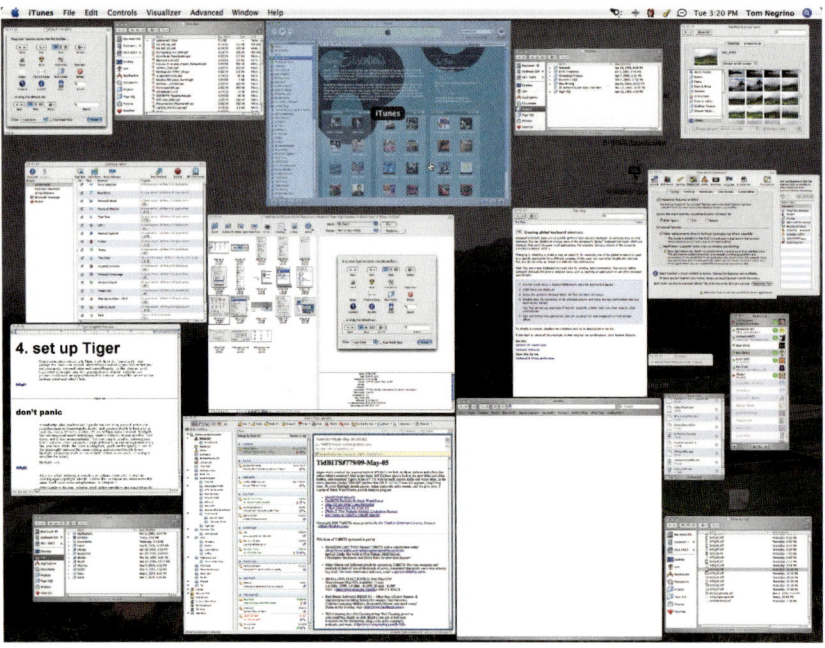

Press F10 to show all the windows for the active application. Press F11 to scoot all windows off the sides of the
screen, exposing the desktop.

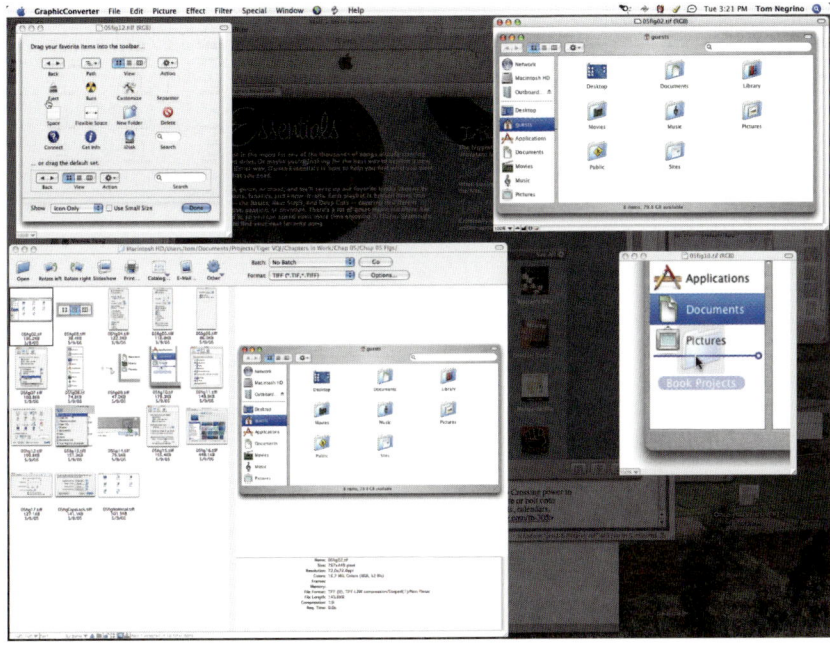

When Exposé is active, you can switch to any of the windows shown by clicking it, or you can navigate through the windows by pressing the arrow keys on
your keyboard, which highlights each window in turn. You can bring a highlighted window to the front and exit Exposé by pressing the Return key, or by
clicking the highlighted window.

Press the shortcut key again to leave Exposé, or you can press the Esc key.

set up exposé (cont.)

Tiger has default shortcut keys set for Exposé, but you can change them if you want, and also set up the hot corners to trigger Exposé. Choose Apple > System Preferences, then click the Dashboard & Exposé icon.

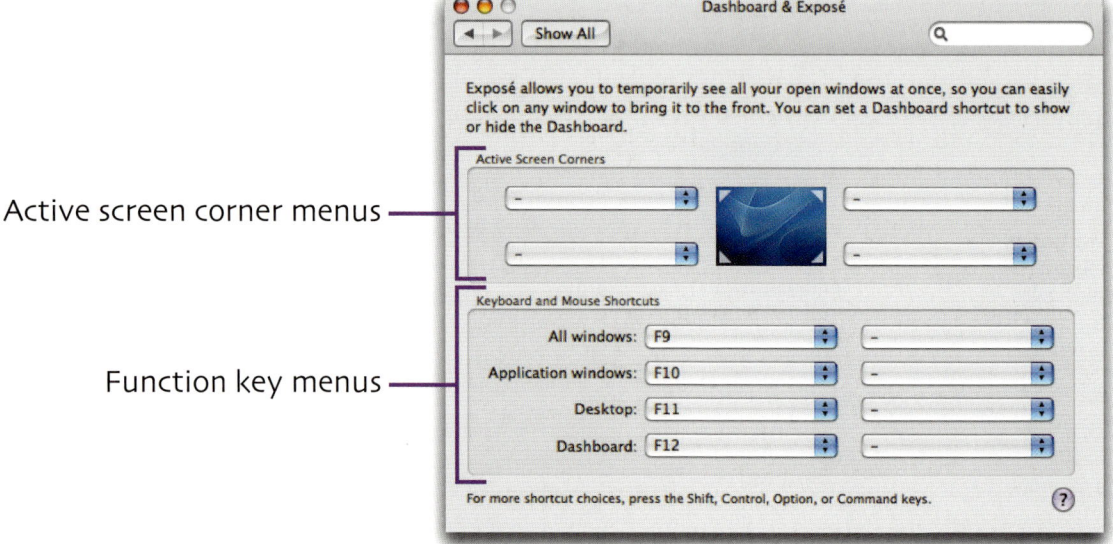

Active screen corner menus ——

Function key menus ——

In the Active Screen Corners section, choose from the pop-up menus if you want a screen corner to be a hot corner that triggers an Exposé action.

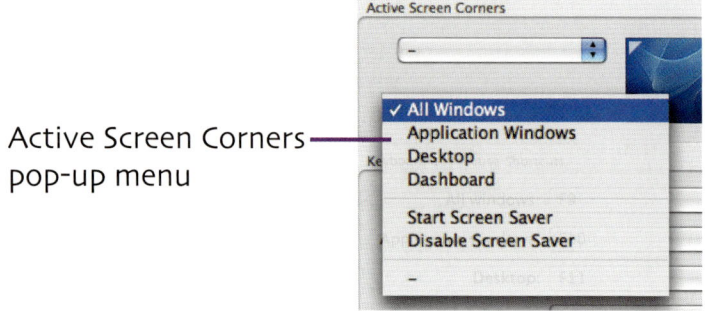

Active Screen Corners
pop-up menu

In the Keyboard and Mouse Shortcuts section, set the function key you want to trigger each Exposé action.

customize your system

set shortcut keys

Tiger has many keyboard shortcuts that are available to you, and it's a good idea to learn at least some of them, as studies have proven that you can be more productive by keeping your hands on the keyboard, rather than using the mouse.

To see what shortcuts are included with the system, choose Apple > System Preferences, then click the Keyboard & Mouse icon, then click the Keyboard Shortcuts tab.

Enable or disable shortcut keys in this column

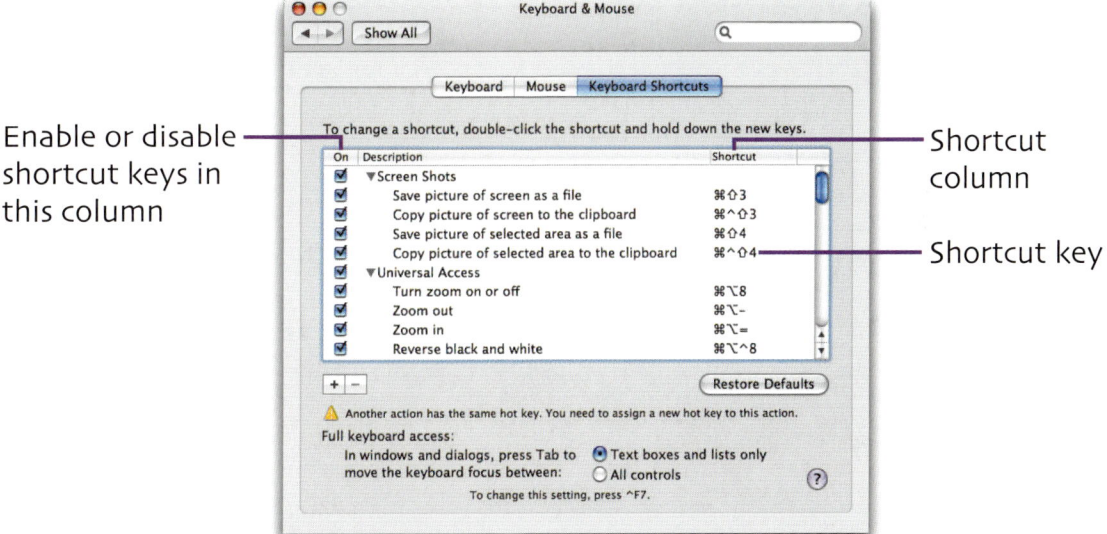

Shortcut column

Shortcut key

You can enable or disable any of the included shortcuts by toggling the On checkbox next to it.

To change a keyboard shortcut, double-click in the Shortcut column, then press the new keys to change the entry.

set shortcut keys (cont.)

One very cool ability of the Keyboard Shortcuts tab is to set keyboard shortcuts for all applications, or for specific applications. That means that you can add a shortcut for a menu item that doesn't usually have one. Let's create a shortcut for Bring All to Front, which brings all the windows of a particular application to the front. This menu item appears in many applications, but it doesn't have a standard keyboard shortcut.

1 In the Keyboard Shortcuts tab, scroll down to the bottom of the list until you see the All Applications item. Select it.

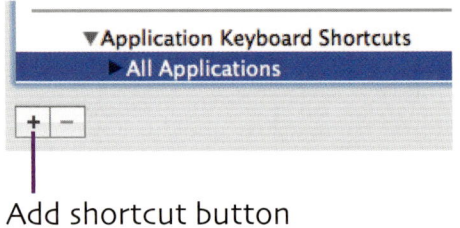

2 Click the Add shortcut button. In the resulting dialog, enter the menu title, in this case Bring All to Front. The name must be exactly the same as the menu title, including upper and lowercase.

Add shortcut button

3 In the Keyboard Shortcut field, press the key combination you want. It helps to use one that you can remember easily, or that is mnemonic. I used Command-F10, because I already know that F10 shows all of an application's windows in Exposé, and I think of Bring All to Front as a related function.

4 Click Add.

You'll need to quit and reopen any running applications to see the resulting change.

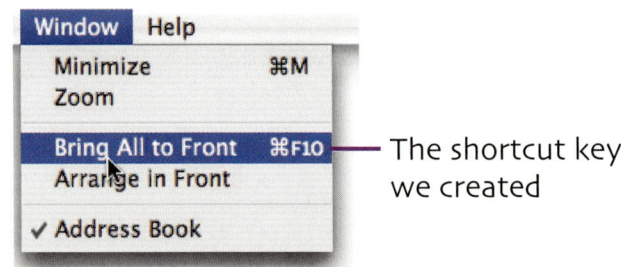

The shortcut key we created

extra bits

customize the sidebar p. 57

- Consider adding folders and even files from your current project to the bottom of your sidebar; it makes it easy to access those files.

- Click and drag icons in the sidebar up or down to rearrange their order.

- You can customize the width of the sidebar by placing the mouse cursor over the border between the sidebar and the main part of window. When the cursor changes to a double-headed arrow, click and drag to set the width.

customize the toolbar p. 59

- You can eliminate the toolbar altogether by clicking the oval button in the upper-right corner of a Finder window. This also eliminates the sidebar and removes the "metal" appearance of the window. This gives you a very clean and uncluttered window, but personally, I don't think the loss of the toolbar and sidebar features are worth it.

set up your desktop p. 61

- Interested in turning off the warning that appears before you empty the Trash? You'll find the appropriate setting by choosing Finder > Preferences, then clicking the Advanced tab. Clear the checkbox next to Show warning before emptying the trash.

extra bits

set shortcut keys p. 67

- If you're like me, you hardly ever use the Caps Lock key. As far as I'm concerned, it's the appendix of the keyboard: a leftover that may have been useful once upon a time (during the Age of Typewriters), but we've evolved beyond it. Worse, it can get in your way, causing you to inadvertently type in all capitals when you don't want to, or cause you grief when typing a password, because you didn't notice it was on. Tiger allows you to change the Caps Lock key and make it work (or not) as you prefer. In the Keyboard & Mouse preferences pane, click the Keyboard tab, then click the Modifier Keys button. In the resulting dialog, change the pop-up menu next to Caps Lock to No Action, which disables the key. Or if you prefer, you can remap the Caps Lock key so that it works like the Command, Option, or Control keys.

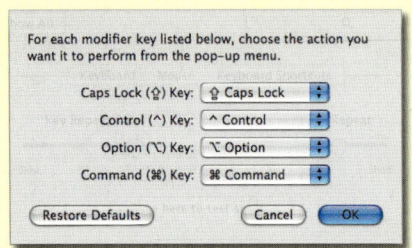

By the way, Tiger will tell you if you have the Caps Lock key on when you try to enter your user password in the login window. The Caps Lock symbol will appear in the password field.

Caps Lock symbol

- You can't set keyboard shortcuts to do common actions like launching programs or switching between applications. For that you'll need a third-party program such as Startly Technologies' QuicKeys X3 (www.startly.com), or Script Software's iKey (www.scriptsoftware.com).

- This isn't a keyboard tip, but it will be useful for left-handed people who have mice with multiple buttons. There's a new option in the Mouse tab of the Keyboard & Mouse preferences pane that allows you to switch the primary mouse button to be the right button, so you can click the primary button with your index finger.

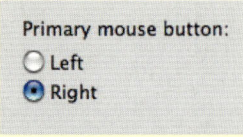

6. learn what's changed

Tiger comes with lots of new features—more than 200 by Apple's count—and many of those can help you do new things, or make it easier or faster to get your work done. Now that you're done with the upgrade, it's time to dig into some of those features.

Tiger's three premier new features are Spotlight, Dashboard, and Automator. I think those are so important that I've devoted separate chapters to each of them, following this one.

In this chapter, we'll take a look at some of Tiger's other improvements, enhancements, and just plain cool new things, and show you how they can enrich your computing experience. But this chapter only scratches the surface of the new enhancements throughout Tiger and its applications; make sure to check out the cool new features in Address Book, iCal, Mail, Text Edit, and QuickTime Player 7.

browse better

Apple's Safari Web browser has added several improvements to its already-excellent abilities. The first thing you'll probably notice is that it is faster; Apple claims it has nearly doubled the speed at which Safari loads and renders Web pages.

Safari now supports RSS, a standard that supplies text descriptions of Web content, along with a link to that content. RSS is widely used by weblogs and news sites to share their latest entries' headlines, synopses, or full text as text streams called feeds. RSS makes it easy to browse the content from one or more sites without having to load their pages.

To view the RSS feed for a site, simply browse to it. If the site offers an RSS feed, the RSS icon will show in Safari's address bar.

Click the RSS icon, and Safari replaces the page with the feed. Some sites provide the entire text of messages, and some only provide the first few lines of the story. On these sorts of sites, you can read the entire text by clicking the Read more links at the end of each entry (or by clicking the story's title). You can also choose to limit the length of the text with the length slider, sort the stories by criteria you choose, or show articles of just a certain vintage.

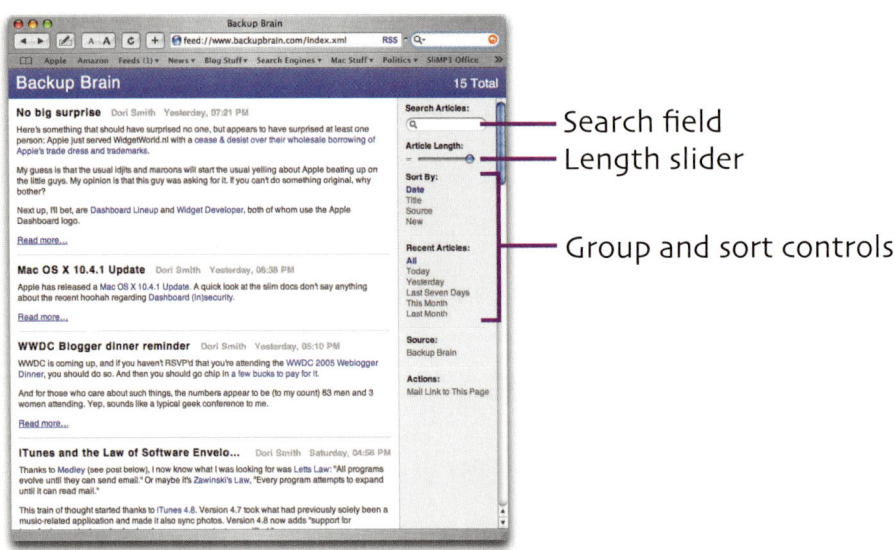

Search field
Length slider

Group and sort controls

learn what's changed

You can now save and email Web pages easily. To save a snapshot of the current page to your hard drive, choose File > Save As, then in the Save dialog, choose Web Archive from the Format pop-up menu, and choose where you want to save the archive. The page, including all of its text and images, will be saved. To view it again, just double-click the Web archive's icon.

This is what the Web archive icon looks like.

To email a Web page, you must be using Apple's Mail as your email program. In Safari, choose File > Mail Contents of This Page. This creates a new Mail message, with the Web page as the content of the message. If you use another mail program, you can instead use File > Mail Link to This Page, which creates a new mail message and enters the URL of the page.

If you have iPhoto 5, part of the iLife '05 package, you can now save images from Safari to iPhoto with one click. Just Control-click on any image and choose Add Image to iPhoto Library from the shortcut menu.

Finally, choose Safari > Private Browsing to keep Safari from adding information to its history, cache, AutoFill, Google searches, and cookies. This allows you to visit sites without leaving any traces on your computer that you did so. You could, for example, use this mode to purchase gifts for family on your home computer, with them being none the wiser until the gift arrived.

look it up!

Words are important. Okay, perhaps it's no surprise that I would think so; after all, words are my business. But Tiger's new Dictionary application is great for anyone who needs to work with words (that would be almost everyone). Dictionary is actually both a dictionary and thesaurus, and it is based on The New Oxford American Dictionary.

Open the Dictionary program, which you'll find in your Applications folder.

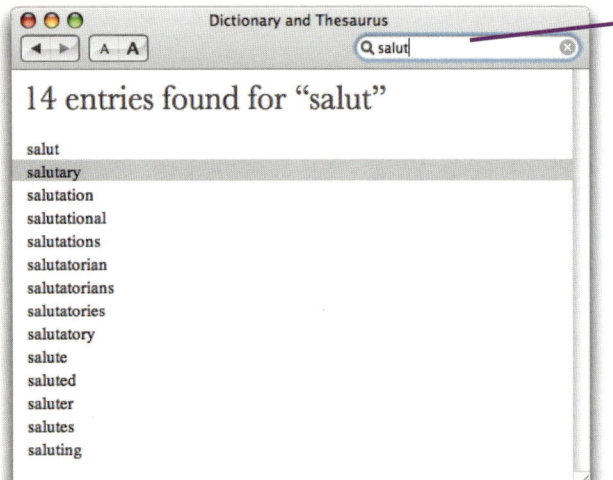

Search field

Enter a word in the search field. As you type, Dictionary searches for matching entries and puts them in the window. If there are multiple matching entries, double-click the one you want, or select it and press Return. The dictionary and (if one exists) the thesaurus entries appear.

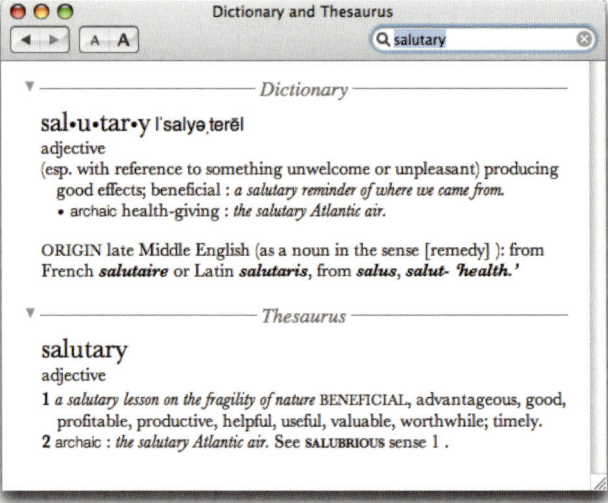

It's a great thing that the Dictionary is integrated throughout the system. It's available to you in most places without even leaving the application you're in. Here's how to bring it up while you're browsing a Web page in Safari, but it works in most applications.

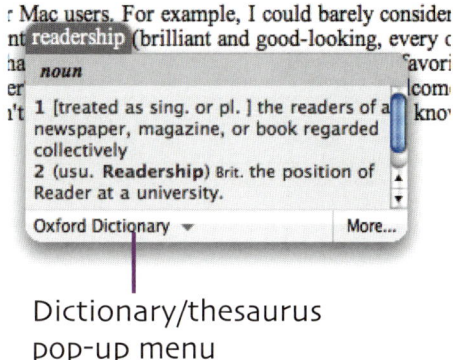

Dictionary/thesaurus pop-up menu

Place the mouse pointer over a word on the page (you don't have to select it), and press Control-Command-D. A Dictionary window pops up with the word's definition.

Choose Oxford Thesaurus from the pop-up menu if you need to see synonyms. Click the More button to open the word in the Dictionary application, which also gives you pronunciation help and word origin information.

But wait, there's one more way to invoke the Dictionary in most applications. This time, select the word that you want to look up, then choose [Application menu] > Services > Look Up in Dictionary. For example, if you're browsing a PDF in the Preview application, select a word and choose Preview > Services > Look Up in Dictionary. The Dictionary application opens and shows you the definition.

use finder features

The Finder has gotten even more useful in Tiger. Besides its improved customization, which you saw in Chapter 5, and its integration with Spotlight, which you'll learn more about in Chapter 7, there are a few other cool new features.

One of my favorites is the new integrated slideshow. To use this, simply select two or more image files in the Finder, then Control-click (right-click if you have a mouse with multiple buttons) and choose Slideshow from the shortcut menu. The slideshow begins, with the images zoomed to fit the screen. At the bottom of the screen you'll find the slideshow controls, which appear when you move the mouse and fade away after a few seconds of inactivity.

Back
Stop/Play
Next
Index Sheet
Actual Size (used in this screenshot)
End Slideshow

learn what's changed

Another feature that is especially useful are the new Burn Folders. These are folders you create that allow their contents to be burned to a recordable or rewritable CD or DVD with the click of a button. This feature is perfect for quick archiving of files that you no longer need on your Mac, or for moving files between two machines.

To create a Burn Folder in the Finder, choose File > New Burn Folder. The new folder appears, ready for you to give it a name. Type the name and press Return or Enter. As you can see, the folder has the CD burning symbol on it.

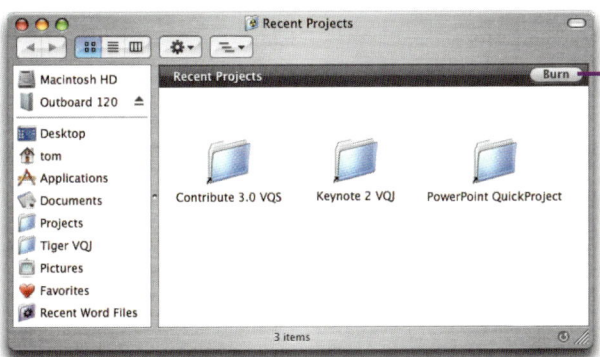

Burn button

Open the Burn Folder, and copy files or folders into the Burn Folder that you want to burn to a disc.

Click the Burn button in the Burn Folder window. The Burn Disc dialog appears, asking you to insert a blank disc. Insert the blank disc, and then a confirmation dialog appears.

Make sure that the name in the confirmation dialog is what you want as the disc's name, then click Burn.

The contents of the folder begin burning to the disc. The Finder keeps you aware of what's going on with a progress dialog. When the burn is complete, the CD appears on your desktop.

learn what's changed

use preview features

With each new version of Mac OS X, Apple has beefed up the Preview application, and Tiger is no exception. This version of Preview allows you to adjust an image's colors; annotate PDF files; capture the screen; and show images in a slideshow.

To edit a picture's colors, open the picture in Preview and choose Tools > Image Correction. The Image Correction palette appears. Adjust the sliders until the picture looks more pleasing; as you move a slider, you see the slider's effect on the picture. In this case, I bumped up the Gamma, Saturation, Contrast, and Sharpness sliders until I liked the effect. If you don't like a change, just click the Reset All button in the palette to bring the settings back to their original values.

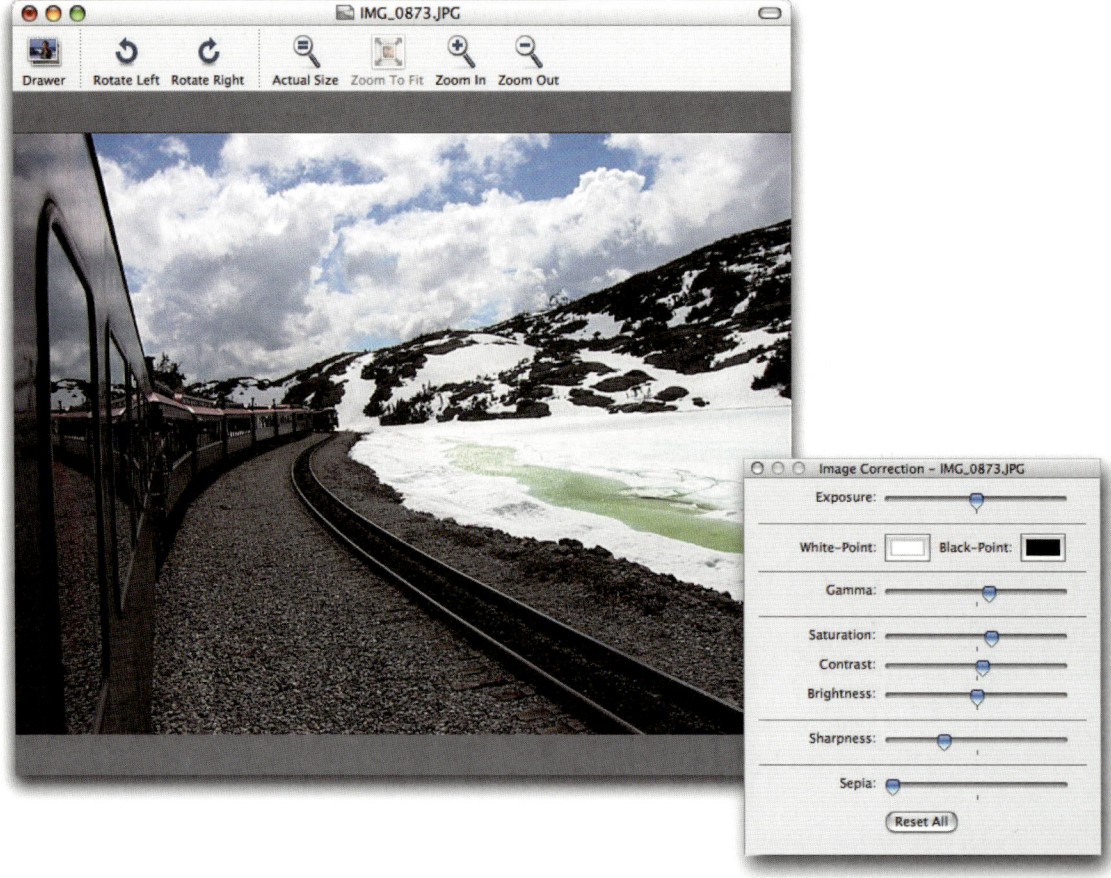

learn what's changed

If you want to annotate a PDF file, begin by opening the file. Then click the new Annotate tool in the toolbar. This tool is a pop-up menu that gives you access to either of the two annotation tools. You can make a text annotation, which puts a yellow sticky note over the document, or you can add a red oval over part of the page. Choose the type of annotation you want, then type (for a text annotation) or draw (for an oval annotation) on the page.

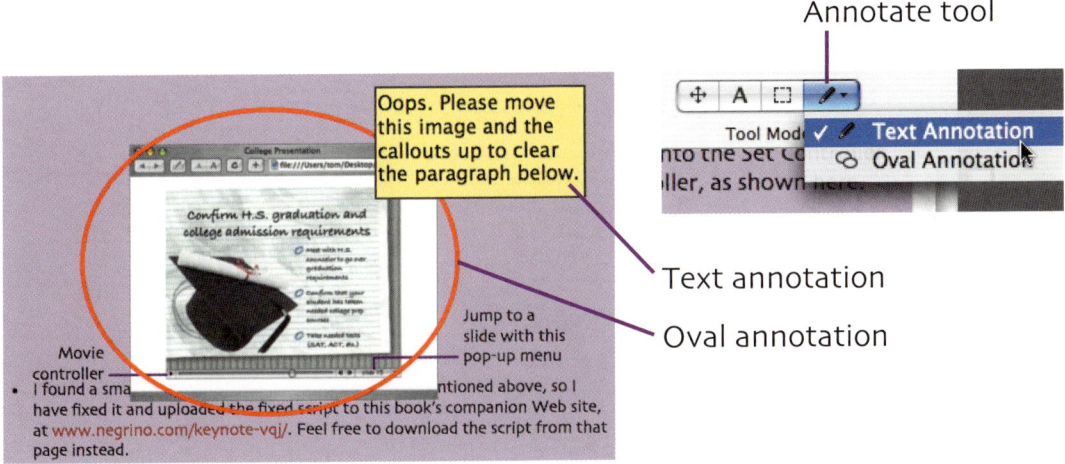

Annotate tool

Text annotation

Oval annotation

You may have used the Grab application to get screenshots in the past, but now Grab's abilities are built into Preview. Choose File > Grab, then choose from the hierarchical menu to grab a Selection, Window, or Timed Screen. The latter choice waits for ten seconds, then takes a picture of the whole screen, which is useful when you need to show things like pull-down menus.

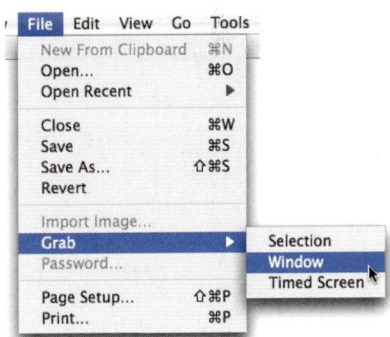

use preview features (cont.)

Preview's new slideshow feature is similar to the slideshow in the Finder, but with an addition. To use it, open a bunch of images by selecting them in the Finder and dragging them onto the Preview icon in your Applications folder or in the Dock. Preview opens, and the files appear in Preview in the Drawer.

Choose View > Slideshow. The slideshow begins. The controls at the bottom of the screen include a button you can use to add the currently displayed image to your iPhoto library.

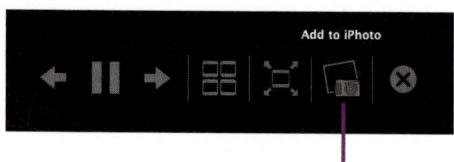

learn what's changed

chat better

The iChat application has some terrific new features, as long as you have hardware powerful enough to support them. Actually, most of the new features don't require more powerful hardware. People who have used AIM (AOL Instant Messaging) know that iChat has lacked some long-standing AIM features, such as buddy groups, multiple chat accounts, and AIM profiles. All of those are now supported. Parents can now set buddy controls for their kids, so you can specify the set of buddies that a child is allowed to chat with.

If you're playing songs from your iTunes library, you can now show the current track that is playing to the world, and people can click the arrow button next to the track name to preview the track in the iTunes Music Store.

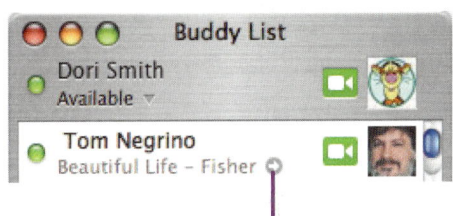

Preview track button

The marquee feature for iChat AV is video chats with as many as four participants, or audio chats with as many as 10 people. The participants in the video chat appear as if they are sitting around a conference table (with their reflections in the tabletop!), and you can see your own video in a small window in the center.

You are here

Add participant button — Mute button

chat better (cont.)

Only people who are using Tiger can participate in multi-person audio or video chats. It's easy to tell which of your buddies are running Tiger, because the sound and video icons will be "stacked," showing they can accommodate more than one person.

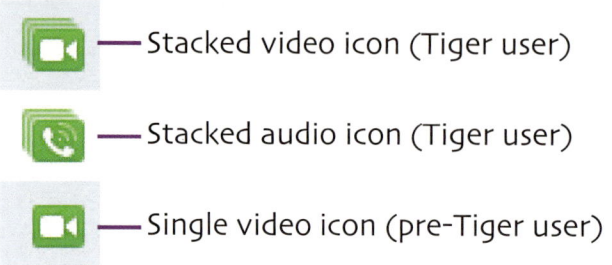

—— Stacked video icon (Tiger user)

—— Stacked audio icon (Tiger user)

—— Single video icon (pre-Tiger user)

To begin a multiple-person audio or video chat, start by selecting one of your buddies that shows a stacked icon in your Buddy List, then click the audio chat or video chat button in the bottom of the Buddy List window.

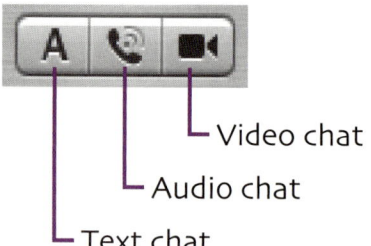

└─ Video chat
└─ Audio chat
└─ Text chat

iChat will initiate the chat. When your buddy responds and the chat begins, click the Add participant (plus) button at the bottom of the chat window, which is actually a pop-up menu that lists the participants in your Buddy List that can be added, i.e., the ones that are showing stacked audio or stacked video icons. iChat will add the new person to the chat. Be sure to see the extra bit on page 84 about the hardware requirements for hosting and participating in a multi-person audio or video chat.

learn what's changed

extra bits

browse better p. 72

- Though Safari can read RSS feeds, it's still no comparison to a dedicated RSS newsreader, such as Ranchero Software's NetNewsWire (www.ranchero. com/netnewswire/), which can fetch and display news from thousands of different sites, making it even easier to keep up with the latest news—or to soak up endless amounts of time reading all that content!

look it up! p. 74

- Tiger's new Dashboard feature also has a Dictionary widget; see Chapter 8 to learn how to open and use widgets.
- Double-clicking on any word that appears in the Dictionary application's definition area looks up that word.

use finder features p. 76

- You may have noticed that when you copy items to the Burn Folder, the Finder does not actually move or make a copy of the items; it just creates aliases to the items and puts the aliases in the Burn Folder. You can tell this because the items in the Burn Folder have the little arrow badge, showing they are aliases. When the folder is burned to disc, the Finder burns the originals of each of the aliased items to the disc.

extra bits

chat better p. 81

- Multi-person video chats have pretty hefty hardware requirements. To begin with, one of the chatters must host and initiate the chat. Apple says that the host must have a Mac with Dual G4 processors, or any G5, plus a broadband Internet connection with at least 384 Kbps in both directions. In the real world, I've found that to get decent-looking video with four people in a video chat, the host should be running a Dual G5 Mac, and have a faster Net connection. Note that this means that no portable Mac shipping as of the time I wrote this (May 2005) could host a video chat. If you have a powerful-enough host, the rest of the participants can get by with less-powerful hardware: a Dual 800 MHz G4, a 1 GHz G4, or any G5, and a broadband Net connection.

- Multi-person audio chats, at least for participants, are within reach of any Mac that can run Tiger. The host needs to have a Dual 800 MHz G4, a 1 GHz G4, or any G5 and a broadband Net connection, but the participants can get by with any G3, G4, or G5 processor and any broadband or even a 56K modem connection.

- iChat AV now uses a video format called H.264 for its video chats, which gives you higher quality video at lower-bit rates. This gives video chats much improved picture quality.

- If you participate in an instant messaging network using the open Jabber protocol, iChat AV now supports Jabber accounts, so you can chat without using a separate Jabber client. To log on to a Jabber network, you'll need to create a Jabber account in iChat first. Choose iChat > Preferences, then click the Accounts button in the toolbar. In the Accounts list, select Jabber Account, then click the Plus button at the bottom of the window. Fill in the account information dialog, and click Add. Close the Preferences window, choose Window > Jabber, and chat away.

learn what's changed

7. use spotlight

Spotlight is the new-in-Tiger system-wide searching technology. Spotlight will change the way that you use your Mac. Sound like a wild claim? Not at all. Just think of all the times that you've tried to find something on your Mac, and failed. Remember how you wasted precious minutes while you looked through file after file. All that frustrated searching is history now.

The genius of Spotlight is that it doesn't just search the names of files and folders; it searches inside documents for words in the file's contents, or for attributes that you specify. You may not have known that files contain all sorts of extra information about their contents. This information is called metadata. For example, when you shoot a picture with your digital camera, the camera also records a bunch of metadata about the image, such as its resolution, the exposure data, when it was shot, and much more. Spotlight knows how to read and search on the metadata for many kinds of files.

When you first boot your machine under Tiger, Spotlight creates an index of the contents of nearly all the files on your machine—Microsoft Word, Excel, and PowerPoint documents, music and movie files, PDFs, your Address Book and iCal entries, e-mail (if you use Apple's Mail program) and more. The index is updated whenever you modify or save a file, so it's always up to date.

use spotlight menu

Getting started with Spotlight is easy; it's right in front of you. New in Tiger is the Spotlight menu at the upper-right corner of your screen. To search for a file or the contents of a file, click the Spotlight icon and the Spotlight menu appears.

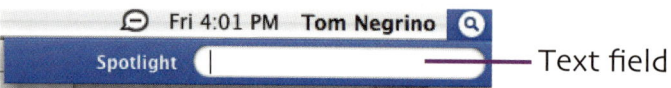 — Text field

Type the search term into the text field. As you type, Spotlight begins its search, changing the menu to show the found items. The more you type, the more refined the search.

As you can see, Spotlight found Word documents, PDFs, images, folders, Safari bookmarks, and even a presentation and MP3 file associated with the search term I used, "tiger." Note that some of the found items do not have "tiger" in their names; Spotlight found the search term inside the files.

To open an item in the list, select it. You can click it in the menu with the mouse, or you can move up and down the menu with the up arrow and down arrow keys. Highlight the item you want, and press the Return or Enter key to open it.

You can also use the system-wide shortcut key combination to get the Spotlight menu. (Command-Space). This drops down the menu and activates its text field, ready for you to begin typing. You can change the shortcut key that activates the Spotlight menu. See "set preferences" later in this chapter.

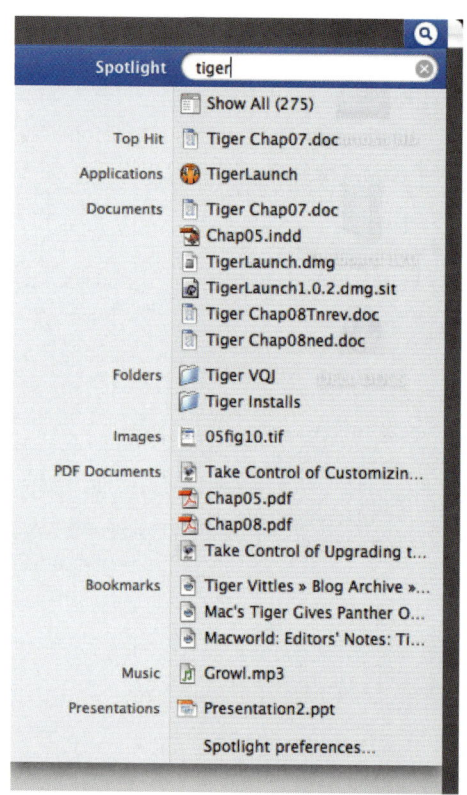

use spotlight window

You may have noticed the topmost entry in the Spotlight menu was Show All with a number after it, and that the number was much larger than the number of entries in the Spotlight menu. That's because Spotlight tries to show you the 20 most-relevant search results in the menu, sorted by kind, and most of the time it's pretty accurate.

But if you need to see all of the results, choose Show All in the Spotlight menu, and the Spotlight window appears.

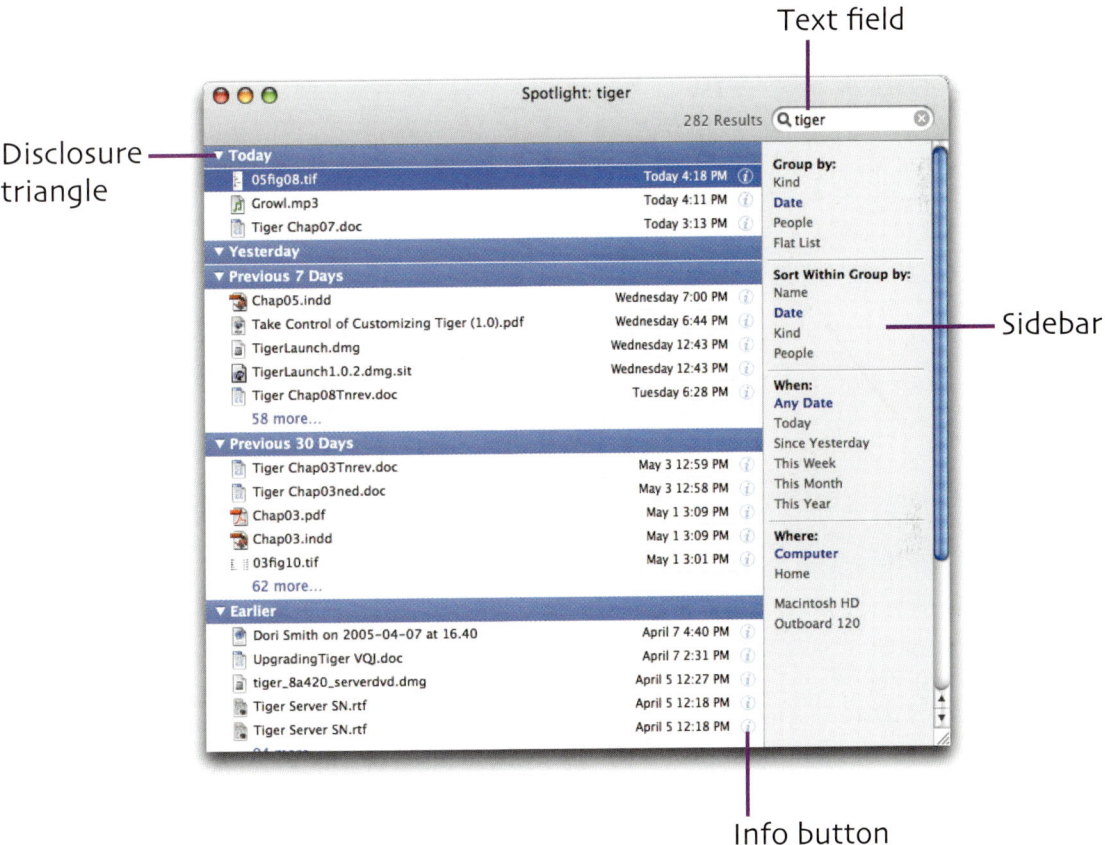

If you need to further narrow your search, this is just the ticket. You can use the grouping and sorting categories in the sidebar to see the search results in a different order, or narrow the results by time or location, just by clicking the links in the sidebar.

use spotlight window (cont.)

You can collapse or expand a category in the window by clicking on its disclosure triangle, just like in Finder list views. If you need to know more about a particular item, click its Info button. Depending on what kind of file it is, you may see a preview of the document (for images and PDFs); a media controller (for sound and video files); or a document icon, along with other information about the item.

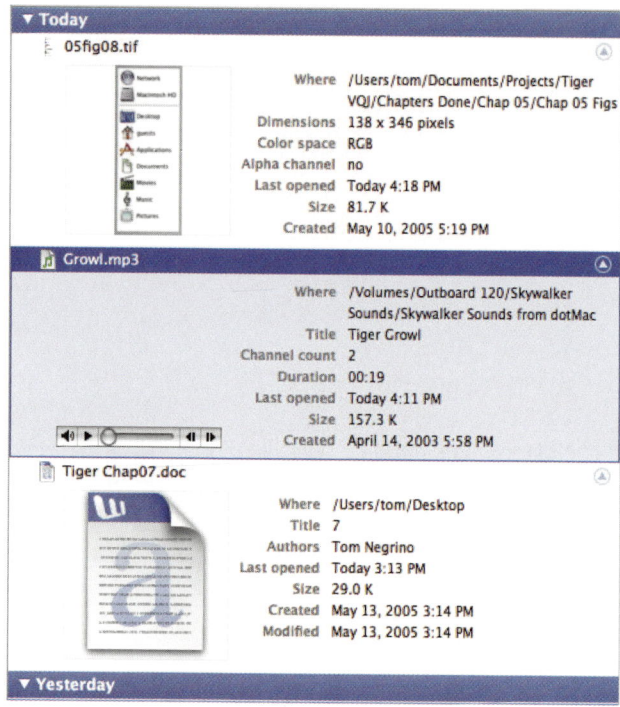

If you group the items by Kind, you'll see additional options for some kinds of documents. For example, the Images category shows you buttons that can display the found images in a full-screen slideshow; display the files as a list; or show you image thumbnails.

View thumbnails

View as list

View slideshow

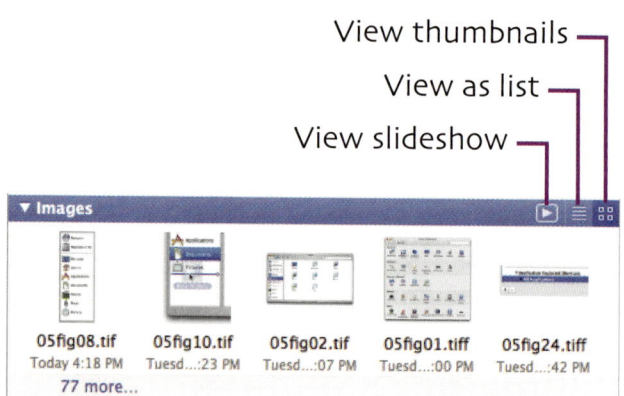

You can also use the system-wide shortcut key combination, which is Command-Option-Space, to bring up the Spotlight window. You can change the shortcut key that activates the Spotlight window. See "set preferences" later in this chapter.

make smart folders

The Finder's Find command has been turbocharged with Spotlight technology, and you can save the searches as Smart Folders, which are automatically (and constantly) updated. You can add a Smart Folder to the sidebar of Finder windows and Open and Save dialogs, and click on it to run the search. Smart Folders are terrific for grouping a bunch of documents that you want to access and work with together, no matter where they actually are on your Mac.

1 Begin by switching to the Finder and choosing File > Find, or pressing Command-F. A New Search window appears.

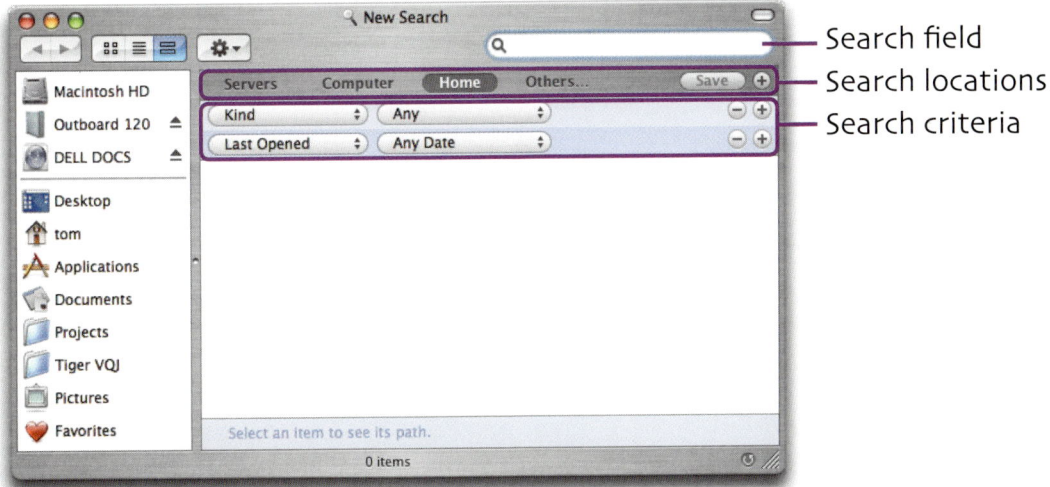

Search field

Search locations

Search criteria

2 If you want to narrow the search, click on one of the search locations.

3 To further narrow the search, choose different search criteria from the pop-up menus. Click the + buttons to add criteria, and remove criteria by clicking the – buttons. As you change criteria, the search updates and results appear in the window. The Others choices in the search criteria pop-up can be used to narrow down your choices quite a bit. In this example, I'm choosing to find Microsoft Word documents that were modified in the last two weeks.

4 To narrow your search further, type a letter or word in the search field.

make smart folders (cont.)

5 To save the search as a Smart Folder, click the Save button. In the resulting dialog, name the Smart Folder, and if you want, choose Add To Sidebar. Click Save.

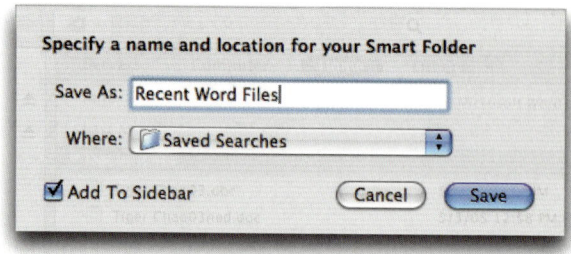

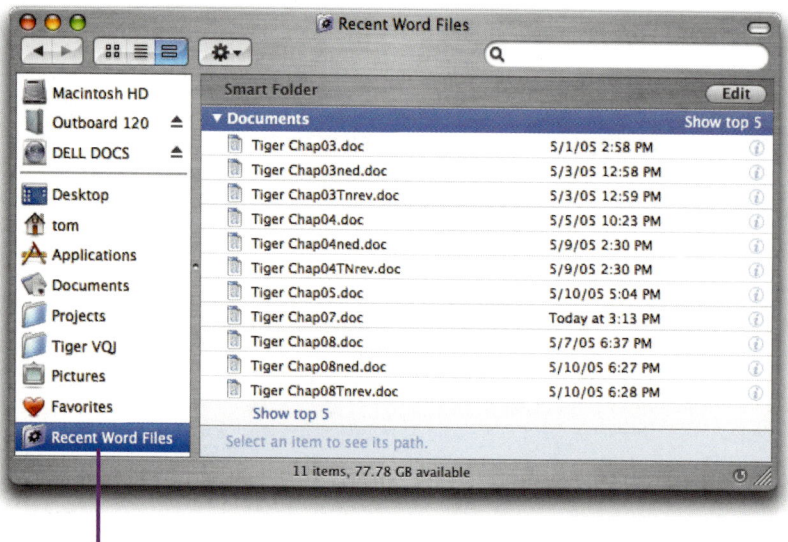

The Smart Folder appears in the sidebar (if you chose that option). To run the search again, click the Smart Folder in the sidebar.

use other spotlights

Spotlight is integrated all over the place in Tiger. Once you begin looking for them, you'll find search fields in many different places, helping you to find all sorts of information faster and easier. Here are some examples:

Finder windows now have a search field and typing in one performs a Spotlight search.

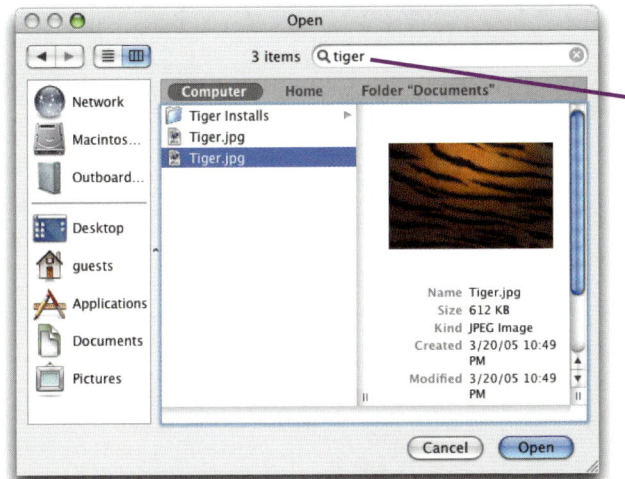

Open and Save dialogs have the Spotlight search field, so it's easier to find documents that you want to, well, open or save.

Need to find a particular bookmark or search your browser history in Safari? Switch to the Safari collections page by choosing Bookmarks > Show All Book-marks, then use the Spotlight search field at the bottom of the window.

In many applications where text is displayed, such as Safari, Preview, or TextEdit, when you select some text and Control-click (or right-click if you have a multiple-button mouse), a contextual menu pops up that allows you to search for that text in Spotlight (or Google, or look it up in the new Dictionary application).

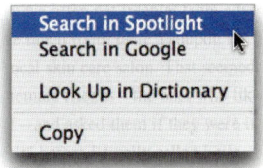

use other spotlights (cont.)

It can be a real pain to try to find a password for a particular Web site. You can get to your stored passwords using the Keychain Access application, which now has a Spotlight search field.

The most literal use of Spotlight will be found in System Preferences, where typing in the search field literally shines a spotlight on the preferences areas that are likely to match what you've typed.

set preferences

You can choose what information will show up in Spotlight's results by setting its preferences. Choose Apple > System Preferences, then click the Spotlight icon. You'll see the search categories that Spotlight uses.

In the Search Results tab, clear the checkboxes for any categories that you don't want to appear in Spotlight search results. You can also drag categories up and down the list, which changes the order in which the results will appear.

To change the keyboard shortcuts for the Spotlight menu or Spotlight window, choose a new shortcut from the pop-up menu, or click in the field and type your new shortcut key. You can also turn the keyboard shortcuts off by clearing the checkboxes.

Shortcut pop-up menus

You can also exclude locations on your hard drives from being searched by Spotlight. Click the Privacy tab.

Click the Add button or drag a folder or disk from the Finder into the list to exclude it from Spotlight searching.

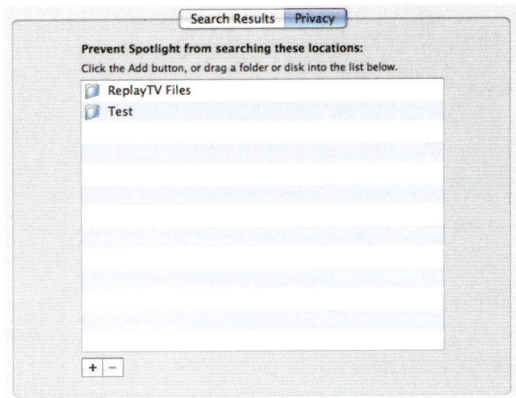

extra bits

use spotlight menu p. 86

- When you first boot into Tiger, Spotlight has to build the initial indexes of your drives. While that's happening, you won't be able to use Spotlight. If you try to use the Spotlight menu, you'll see a progress indicator.

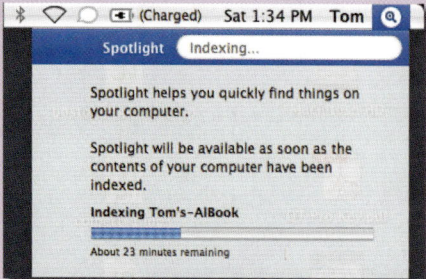

- The contents of some files can't yet be searched by Spotlight, because their applications will need to be updated in order to allow Spotlight to index their documents, or because the applications' creators will have to write a plug-in for Spotlight that teaches Spotlight how to search inside. For example, Microsoft Entourage uses a database to store its information, and Spotlight couldn't index the database's contents when I wrote this (though Microsoft said they were working on the problem). But even with files that Spotlight can't look inside, it can still find those files by their names.

use spotlight window p. 87

- You can make your search results more relevant by adding Spotlight comments to a file's Get Info window in the Finder. Select a file and choose File > Get Info. Enter a keyword or phrase into the Spotlight Comments field. You can easily add the same comment to many different files in one step using an Automator action. See Chapter 9 for more about Automator.

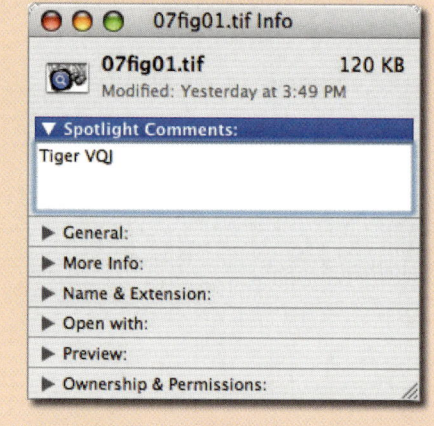

make smart folders p. 89

- If you click on an item in the Search window, you can see the path to the item at the bottom of the window.

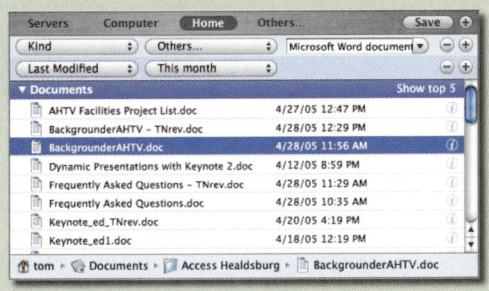

- If you choose not to save the Smart Folder in the Sidebar, you'll find it in ~/Library/Saved Searches/.

use other spotlights p. 91

- In Address Book, select a contact, then choose Spotlight contact name from the Action menu. You'll see a Spotlight window with all documents, iCal appointments, emails (if you use Apple's Mail program), and much more.

- In the Spotlight search in System Preferences, the area that Spotlight thinks is most likely to match your search term shows the brightest spotlight.

8. discover dashboard

The concept behind Dashboard is new but easy to understand: it's like an alternate desktop, containing small mini-applications called widgets. Widgets are tiny self-contained applications that do one small, simple thing. Apple ships a number of widgets with Tiger. Some of them display the weather, show stock prices, look up words in the system's dictionary or thesaurus, control iTunes, serve as a calculator, and more.

These widgets appear in the Dashboard layer, which is a semi-transparent window that covers your whole screen. When the Dashboard layer is visible, you can use widgets; when Dashboard is hidden, the widgets are whisked off your screen and out of view. Widgets are great for information you need for a moment, then you can continue with your work. For example, if you're setting up a lunch date and want to check the weather forecast for next Tuesday, just call up Dashboard. Or you can use the calculator widget to add a few numbers while you're on a phone call.

In this chapter, you'll learn how to access Dashboard and use widgets; set Dashboard preferences; and install widgets from the large number of third-party widgets that have appeared since Tiger's release.

trigger dashboard

By default, you press the F12 key on your keyboard or click the Dashboard icon in the Dock to make the Dashboard layer appear. If you want to change Dashboard's function key, you can; see set preferences later in this chapter.

Dashboard icon

The Dashboard layer appears, with any open widgets appearing to zoom in from off the screen. If you're used to Exposé changing the way your desktop appears, switching to and from the Dashboard layer should quickly feel like second nature.

By default, four widgets are open: the calculator, an analog clock, a calendar, and a weather forecast display.

To leave the Dashboard layer, press F12 again, click the Dashboard icon in the Dock, or click anywhere on the desktop that isn't covered by a widget.

use widgets

Widgets are a little odd, in that they all look different, they can be any arbitrary shape, and they don't have familiar user interface controls such as window title bars or close buttons. For longtime Mac users, they're fun to look at, but a little jarring.

But many widgets do share some user interface conventions. Open the Dashboard layer and look at the weather widget again. Now move your mouse pointer over the widget. You'll see that a small italic i appears in the lower-right corner of the widget. That's the info button, which allows you to set a widget's preferences.

Info button

Many widgets have info buttons, but some do not (because they don't need preferences, such as the calculator widget).

Click the info button. With a neat animated effect, the widget spins on its vertical axis and shows you its "back" side, which allows you to set preferences for the widget. In the case of the weather widget, you can enter a city and state or a ZIP code to set your location.

use widgets (cont.)

When you've entered the new location, click the Done button. The widget spins back around to show you its "front," and the weather in the new location appears. To see a six-day forecast, click anywhere on the widget except for the info button.

This trick of clicking on a widget to toggle what it is displaying is a common one. For example, clicking on the Calendar widget hides and shows the month, leaving only the day and date.

You can move a widget on your screen by clicking and dragging anywhere on the widget that isn't a button or a form field. You don't have to click in a particular area, like you do with a regular window.

control dashboard

You can open more widgets from the Widget Bar, which is normally hidden. To bring up the Widget Bar, click the Widget Bar toggle, which is the odd "plus inside a circle" transparent icon floating in the bottom-left corner of your screen.

When you do this, you'll see several things happen:

- The Widget Bar moves up from the bottom of the screen, pushing the rest of the desktop up and partly off the top of the display, so the regular menu bar is no longer visible. The Widget Bar looks like a gray metal grill with holes in it, and contains scroll arrows to the left and right so you can see more widgets.

- Widgets appear in the Widget Bar, starting from the left and displaying in alphabetical order.

- Any widgets already visible now display a close button, which is an X inside a circle.

- A semi-transparent button saying "More Widgets…" appears on the right side of the screen, just above the Widget Bar.

- If your Dock is positioned on the left or right side of the screen, the top icon (or two) appears to be off the top of the screen. If your Dock is positioned on the bottom, the Dock moves up, just above the Widget Bar.

- The Widget Bar toggle itself changes from a plus inside a circle to an X inside a circle, indicating that you can click it to close the Widget Bar.

Scroll arrow ⌐   Scroll arrow ¬

control dashboard (cont.)

To launch a widget, click that widget's icon in the Widget Bar. If you have a sufficiently powerful graphics card in your Mac, you'll see the widget appear with a nifty rippling water visual effect.

Close button

To close a widget, click its close button. The widget will disappear with some more eye candy, looking as though it is being sucked into the close button.

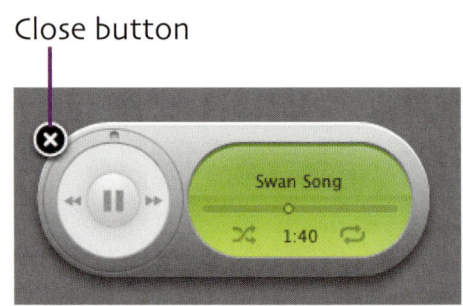

To view more widgets, move the cursor over one of the scroll arrows on either side of the Widget Bar. The arrow changes to a small button, telling you both how many Widget Bars full of widgets you have and which bar you're currently on. Click the arrow and the next bar of widgets (in alphabetical order) will display.

If you want more widgets (and who among us does not?), click the More Widgets button. You'll leave the Dashboard layer and your Web browser will take you to Apple's Dashboard site, where you can check out and download additional widgets.

To hide the Widget Bar, click the Widget Bar toggle in the lower-left, just above the Widget Bar. You'll still be in the Dashboard layer, but the Widget Bar is now hidden, and the widgets themselves no longer display close boxes. Alternately, you can just leave the Dashboard layer, and when you next return, the Widget Bar will be hidden.

discover dashboard

set preferences

Because Apple added Dashboard's preferences to the Exposé preference pane of System Preferences, it's natural to think that the two have something in common, but they're about as related as your Desktop picture and your screen saver are to each other—i.e., not at all, except in the most general sense.

Choose Apple > System Preferences, then click the Dashboard & Exposé icon.

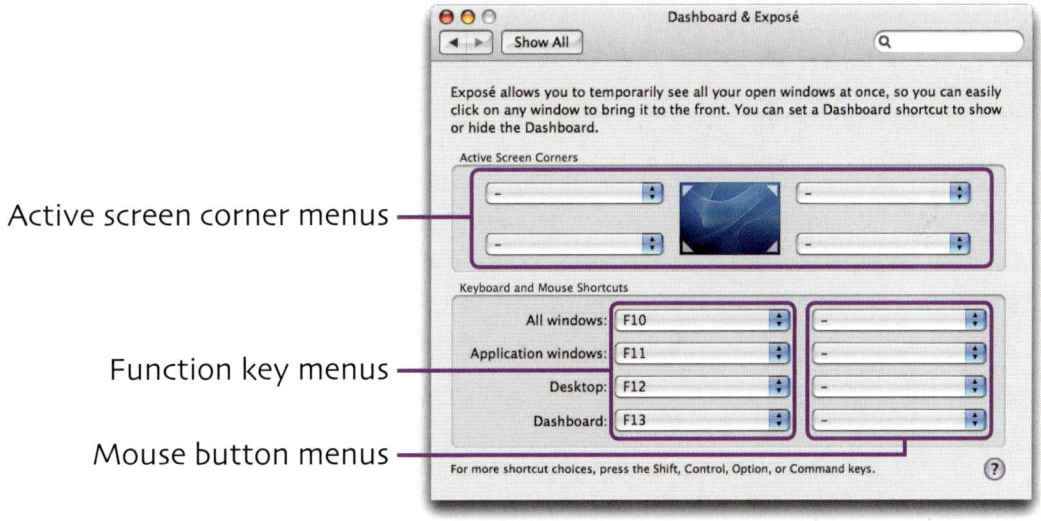

Active screen corner menus ——

Function key menus ——

Mouse button menus ——

In the Active Screen Corners section, choose from the pop-up menus if you want a screen corner to be a hot corner that triggers an Exposé action, Dashboard, or the screen saver.

In the Keyboard and Mouse Shortcuts section, set the function key you want to use to trigger Dashboard (you can use F1 through F13). As you can see, I was already used to using F12 to trigger Exposé in Panther, so I changed Dashboard to use F13 instead of the default F12. You can also use the mouse button menus for additional choices, if you have a mouse or trackball with more than one button.

install new widgets

You're probably going to want more widgets than the ones Apple ships with Tiger, and many more started appearing from third-party developers as soon as Tiger shipped. You can download them from Apple's Dashboard site, at www.apple.com/macosx/dashboard/, or you can pick from one of the Dashboard Web sites you'll find listed at www.dori.com/dashboard/.

Widgets live on your system in one of two places. Widgets that are shared by all the users of your machine are inside /Library/Widgets/. That is, double-click the icon of your hard disk in the Finder, open the Library folder, and you'll find the shared Widgets folder inside.

Each user on your Mac (if you have multiple users enabled; see Chapter 4 for more information) can also have their own set of personal widgets, which are in ~/Library/Widgets/. To find that folder, open your Home folder, then the Library folder, and you'll find your personal Widgets folder. When you trigger Dashboard, you'll see both sets of widgets.

Apple's done a little behind-the-scenes magic to make downloaded widgets install themselves: if the site's done their work correctly, you should just be able to click on a link in Safari and download the widget, and the widget will move itself into ~/Library/Widgets/. From there, it will automatically appear on the Widget Bar the next time you're in the Dashboard layer.

If a site hasn't set up its widget correctly for download, you may have to move it manually into ~/Library/Widgets/.

extra bits

trigger dashboard p. 98

- You can also bring up the Dashboard layer by using one of the screen hot corners you set in preferences, or by double-clicking a widget file.

- You can also leave the Dashboard layer by moving the cursor to the screen hot corner that you chose in preferences, or by clicking a widget that calls an application. For instance, clicking the red button in Apple's Address Book widget launches the Address Book application, makes it active, and leaves the Dashboard layer.

use widgets p. 99

- You will need an active Internet connection to get the weather from the weather widget. Many other widgets similarly rely on an active Net connection.

- The weather widget shows you the weather conditions with a graphic in the widget. You can see each of the built-in graphics, by holding down the Option and Command keys and clicking the graphic. Every time you click, the image will change to a different weather condition. You probably also noticed that the location changed to Nowhere. Leave the Dashboard layer and open it again to get your location back.

- I like to group widgets on my screen so that widgets that primarily display information are in one corner of the screen, and widgets that require typing, such as the dictionary, address book, and phone book widgets, are closer to the center of the screen.

continues on next page

extra bits

- You can close a widget without opening the Widget Bar by holding down the Option key and moving the mouse pointer over the widget. The widget's close button will appear.

- If you want multiple instances of the same widget, just click it again. For example, you can have two Stickies widgets, each with a different color, font, and text.

- When launching a widget, be aware that each one will launch in the exact same spot. You may not realize that you've clicked on the Stickies widget three times, for example, as you can only see the top-most Sticky. After you launch a widget, move it from the default location, and then you'll be able to see if you've launched more than one.

control dashboard p. 101

- There's an undocumented keyboard shortcut to open and close the Widget Bar. Rather than clicking the plus in a circle icon, you can press Command-= (Command and the equals key). You must use the equals key on the main part of the keyboard, not the one on the numeric keypad.

set preferences p. 103

- If you hold down the Shift, Control, Option, or Command keys (or any combination of them) while setting the active screen corners, keyboard, or mouse shortcut pop-up menus, you can use them as part of the command. For example, let's say that you're used to using F12 for Exposé. You can change the Dashboard trigger command to Control-F12.

install new widgets p. 104

- Interested in building your own widgets? They're not that hard to create, if you have a little Web design experience. Widgets are created using HTML, CSS, and JavaScript, which you also use to make Web pages. To learn more about making widgets, I recommend that you pick up Dashboard Widgets for Mac OS X Tiger : Visual QuickStart Guide, by Dori Smith.

9. save time with automator

For a moment, reflect on the reason you use a computer. It's so that you can get your work done faster and easier, isn't it? Or so you can do things that you couldn't do at all without a computer? So let me ask you another question: why do we put up with computers that are so dumb that we have to walk them through the same tasks over and over again? I've spent countless hours doing repetitive dogwork like making identical modifications to a bunch of different images. Other times there are things that I don't do with my computer, because I know they will take too long and be too tedious.

Apple has tried to solve this problem before, when it created the AppleScript programming language. AppleScript allows you to write programs that can automate tasks in a single application, or make two or more applications work together to do what you want. But the problem is that most people don't want to learn a programming language, so until now, there wasn't a good way for regular people to automate tasks.

Tiger's new Automator application takes the hassle and pain out of automating a task. In Automator, you take a sequence of steps (which in Automator-speak, are called actions) and assemble them into a workflow. You can mix and match actions from different applications, and creating a workflow requires exactly zero programming ability. It's really easy. You can save a workflow as a document, so once you have created a workflow, you can run it again anytime.

In this chapter, you'll learn how to create a couple of sample workflows, and see how Automator can save you tons of time and banish boring tasks.

build a workflow

The first thing you need to do to build a workflow is obvious, but important. Ask yourself two questions: first, what is it that you want to do? And second, what steps are required to accomplish the task? Each of those steps will be an Automator action, and you'll string them together into your workflow.

Open Automator (it's in your Applications folder). An untitled Automator window appears.

The Search Actions field allows you to find actions quickly.

The Run button runs the workflow.

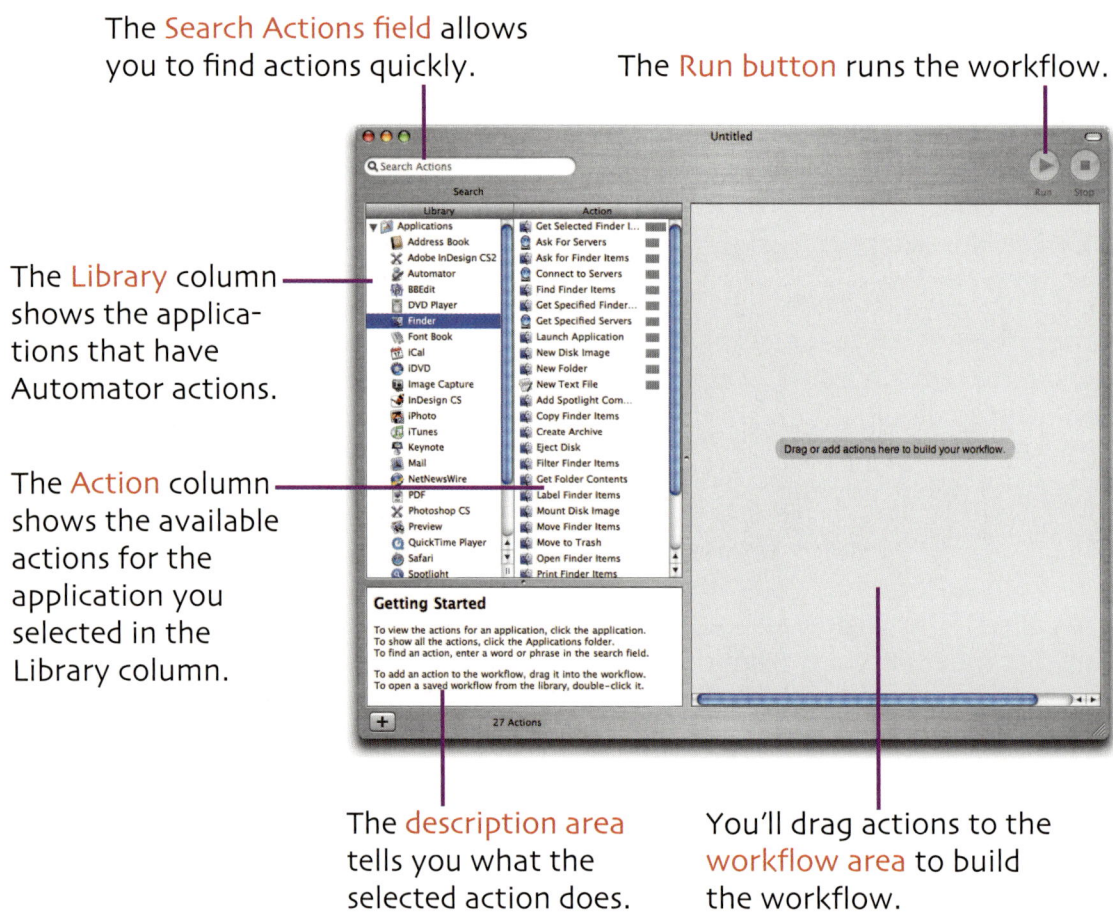

The Library column shows the applications that have Automator actions.

The Action column shows the available actions for the application you selected in the Library column.

The description area tells you what the selected action does.

You'll drag actions to the workflow area to build the workflow.

The example workflow we'll build here does something that is both useful and would be an incredible pain to do by hand. Like many people, I've purchased music from the iTunes Music Store (iTMS). Because I've spent money on these songs, they're valuable to me, and I'd like to make sure they're backed up to a recordable CD in case of a computer failure. But these files are scattered among many different folders inside my iTunes music library folder, and it would take forever to open all those folders and copy the purchased song files. So we'll build a workflow that finds just the purchased songs from the iTMS, copies them to a new folder, then burns them to a CD.

1 Because copying files and burning a CD can be time-consuming, we'll put up a confirmation dialog at the beginning of the workflow, to make sure it wasn't run by mistake. Click the Automator entry in the Library column, then drag Ask for Confirmation from the Action column to the workflow area.

2 In the Message field, type the name of the workflow, then in the Explanation field, type a description of the workflow. You can also click into the buttons and change their text; I changed the default OK button to Continue.

Message field —

Explanation field —

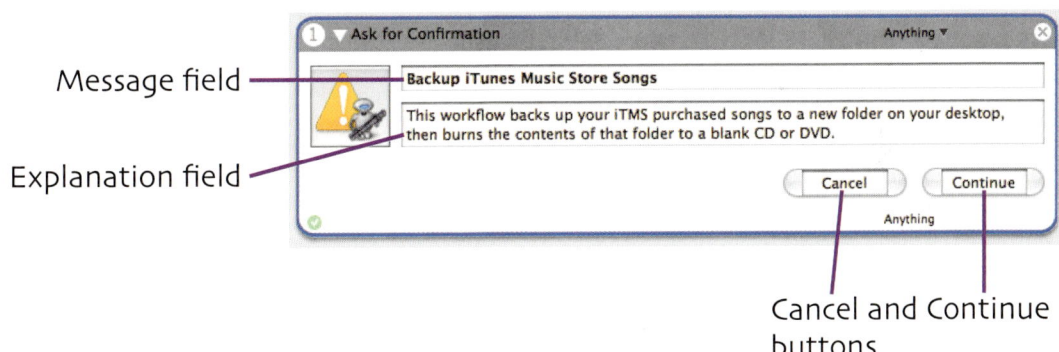

Cancel and Continue buttons

build a workflow (cont.)

3 Now we'll add an action that finds the iTMS songs. Click the Spotlight entry in the Library column, then drag Find iTunes Items from the Action column to the workflow area, below the Ask for Confirmation action. In the Find pop-up menu, choose Songs. In the Whose section, choose Kind from the first pop-up menu, choose Contains from the second pop-up menu, and type Protected in the text field (songs bought from the iTMS have the kind MPEG-4 Audio File (Protected)).

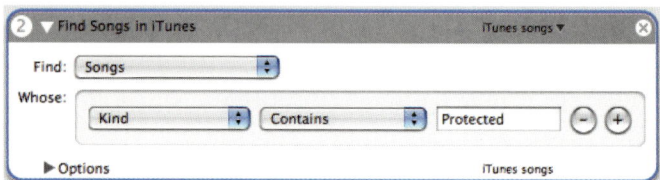

4 The next step is to create a new folder that will eventually contain the files that the last step found. Click the Finder entry in the Library column, then drag New Folder from the Action column to the workflow area. In the Name field, type "iTMS Songs", and choose Desktop from the Where pop-up menu. Notice that this action is taking some information that was passed to it from the previous action, in this case the iTunes songs that the last action found. Automator shows information passed from one action to another as connections between actions.

Name field   Connection showing passed information

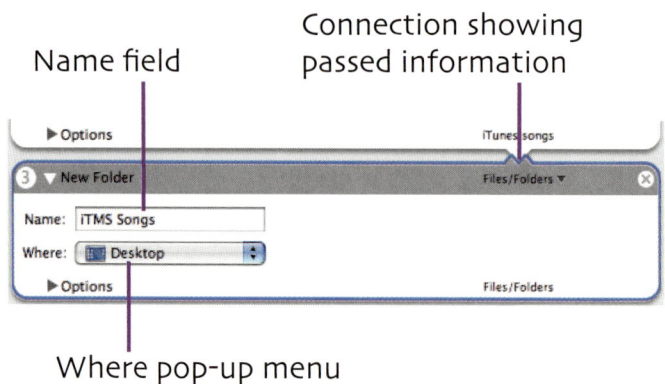

Where pop-up menu

5 Now we want to copy the iTunes songs to the new folder. Click the Finder entry in the Library column, then drag Copy Finder Items

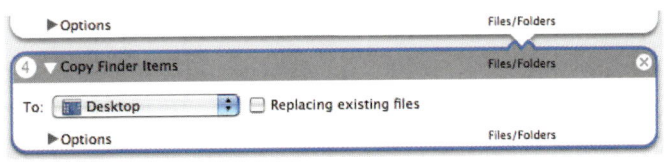

from the Action column to the workflow area. As you can see, it's connected to the previous action, indicating that it will accept the information passed to it (which are the names of the found iTunes songs).

6 The final step is to burn the files that were copied to the new folder to a recordable CD. Click the System entry in the Library column, then drag Burn a Disc from the Action column to the workflow area. In the Disc Name field, type

iTMS Backup, then click the Append date checkbox and clear the Erase first checkbox. The defaults in the After Burning section are fine. It's not a bad idea to get another confirmation before burning a disc, so click the Options disclosure triangle and check Show Action When Run.

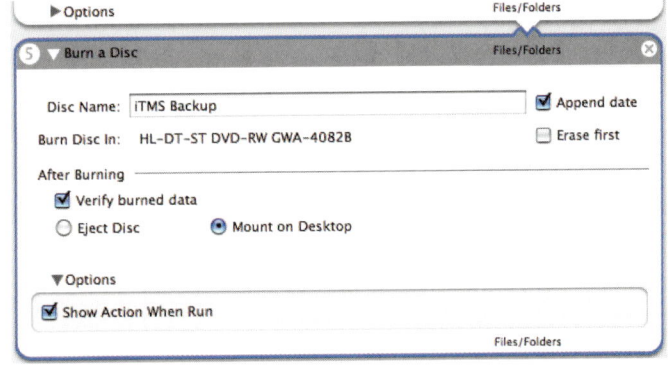

Congratulations; you're done with your workflow. Here's what all the steps look like together (I've collapsed the steps to their titles for easier viewing).

build a workflow (cont.)

To run the workflow, click the Run button at the top of the window. The workflow runs, first showing you the confirmation dialog.

The workflow continues, finding the protected files and copying them to the new folder on the desktop, then it gives you the Burn a Disc confirmation dialog.

Put a blank disc in your Mac, click the Continue button, and the folder with the protected music files will be burned to the CD or DVD. When the disc is done, it will appear on your desktop.

save your workflow

You can save your workflow in three ways. You can save it as a workflow document, which can be run or edited from within Automator. It can be saved as an application, so you can double-click and run it from the Finder or the Dock or any other method you use to run an application. Finally, you can save the workflow as a plug-in, which allows your workflow to appear in, and run from, an application you select. See the extra bit about where it's best to use each kind of saved workflow.

You should save your workflows in ~/Library/Workflows/. This makes them appear in the My Workflows folder in the Automator Library column.

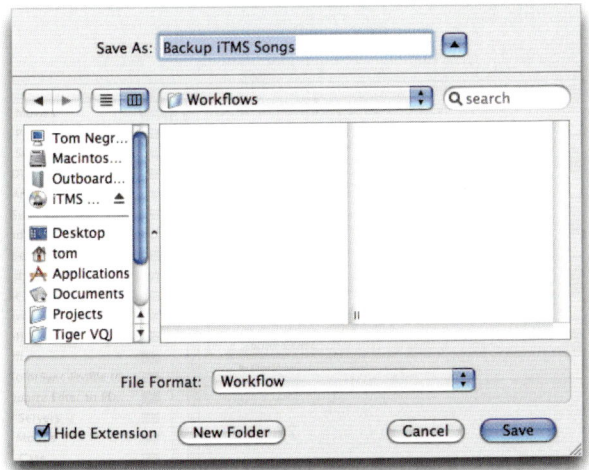

To save a workflow document, create a workflow in Automator, then choose File > Save. The Save dialog will appear. Navigate to ~/Library/Workflows/. From the File Format pop-up menu, choose Workflow.

To save a workflow as an application, choose File > Save. The Save dialog will appear. Navigate to wherever you want to save the application. From the File Format pop-up menu, choose Application. The workflow will appear in the Finder as an Automator application.

save your workflow (cont.)

To show how to save and use a workflow as a Finder plug-in, we'll first create a short workflow that will allow you to add Spotlight comments to selected files in the Finder (see Chapter 7 for more about Spotlight).

1 In Automator, choose File > New.

2 Click the Finder entry in the Library column, then drag Get Selected Finder Items from the Action column to the workflow area.

3 Now drag Add Spotlight Comments to Finder Items from the Action column to the workflow area. Leave the New Spotlight Comments field blank.

Click the Options disclosure triangle, then check Show Action When Run. When the workflow is run, this will make Automator present us with a dialog into which we can enter the Spotlight comments. The workflow is complete.

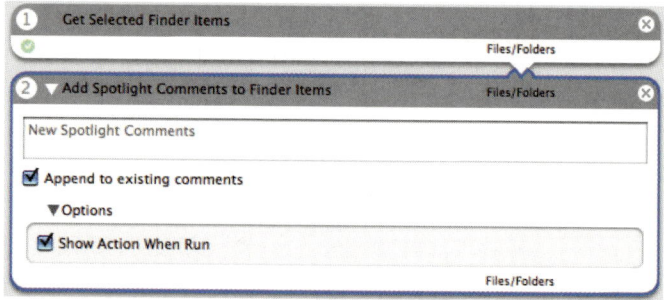

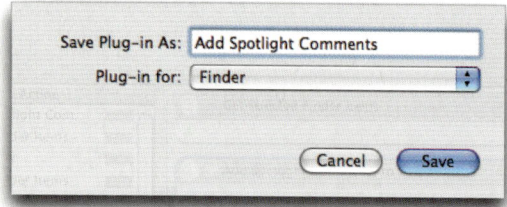

4 Choose File > Save As Plug-In. In the resulting dialog, name the plug-in and choose Finder from the Plug-in for pop-up menu. Then click Save.

To use the plug-in workflow, select one or more files in the Finder, then Control-click (or right-click if you have a multiple-button mouse). In the shortcut menu that pops up, you'll see an Automator item, with a hierarchical menu with your new plug-in listed. Choose it, and the workflow will run.

extra bits

build a workflow p. 108

- You can change the order of actions in the workflow area by dragging them up or down.

- Not all applications have Automator actions, but many do, and many others are being updated to include Automator actions. Check the manufacturer's Web site to see if they have actions available, and also do a Google search for the application's name and "Automator action". You'll find that many sites are creating Automator actions and workflows for popular applications, such as Adobe Photoshop and InDesign.

- You can see a file's Kind by selecting the file in the Finder and choosing File > Get Info.

- Information passed from one action to another is passed sequentially through the steps of the workflow, from top to bottom.

- Workflows, at least in Automator 1.0, are relatively simple. The workflow begins at the top of the window, and actions execute in the order that they were added to the workflow, one right after another. There is no "If...Then" logic that changes the workflow if a particular situation occurs during the workflow. For example, imagine that you had a workflow that automatically sends emails, but that when you ran the workflow, your Net connection was down. The workflow will fail, but you won't necessarily know it. A bit of program logic could put up a dialog that lets you know that the emails weren't sent.

- You can find more news and workflows that other people have created at Automator World (www.automatorworld.com), as well as Apple's Automator site (www.automator.us).

save time with automator

extra bits

save your workflow p. 113

- You use the different methods of saved workflow in different situations. The saved workflow document is good to use when you want to run workflows from within Automator, perhaps because you might want to edit the workflow to tweak it to do exactly what you want. The workflow saved as an application works best for workflows that you want to be able to run by double-clicking them in the Finder, or from the Dock. For example, I have a workflow that I used for this book, which when double-clicked, opened a template file and a library file in Adobe InDesign, then placed the Microsoft Word file into the InDesign layout. When I finished writing this chapter, I simply double-clicked the workflow, and part of the layout job was done automatically (I still had to insert all the graphics and adjust the text flow around the graphics). You use the plug-in style of workflow for operations on items that you want to select and work with directly. For example, if you have workflows that begin by working on icons selected in the Finder, making the workflow a Finder plug-in is the most efficient way to get the workflow started.

10. terrific additions for tiger

The rest of this book tells you why Mac OS X 10.4 Tiger is great. But it's still not perfect; there's always more that people want from their computing experience. Happily, there are a slew of add-on applications and utilities that can customize and enhance your Mac to a tee.

Writing about all of these applications and system enhancements could easily take another entire book, so I'm just going to mention some of the ones that are among the most popular. Because these things are subjective, I'm not going to prescribe which utility to use in a particular category. Instead, I'll give you a few choices to try out. Many of the programs are free, and the rest are demo-ware (you can use the program for a while, typically 30 days, to try it out, after which you must pay to continue using it).

You can find and keep track of the latest versions of Mac programs at two Web sites. VersionTracker (www.versiontracker.com) and MacUpdate (www.macupdate.com) keep up-to-date lists of virtually all software released for the Mac platform, and you can search the sites to find information about programs, information about developers, and links to download software.

use a launcher

One of the things that we do most often with our computers is to launch applications or documents. Several of Mac OS X's features are designed to help you access and launch items, such as the Finder, the Dock, and new in Tiger, Spotlight. Each of these has its place, but they all have limitations, too. These launching utilities try to work around those limitations.

Simple and free, Ranchero Software's TigerLaunch adds a system-wide menu to your menu bar that lists the applications you use the most. You choose the applications that appear on the menu via an easy configuration dialog. www.ranchero.com/software/

If you like the Dock, but feel that it just doesn't go far enough and isn't customizable enough, DragThing, from TLA Systems, is just the ticket. It gives you as many docks as you want, into which you can place applications, documents, folders, or URLs. It also has docks for all running applications, all mounted disks, or all open windows. DragThing is incredibly customizable, and has far too many features for me to list. $29. www.dragthing.com

For people who are more keyboard-oriented, two launching utilities, LaunchBar and QuickSilver, stand out. The idea behind these programs is that you hit a hotkey to bring them up, type a few letters, and the program gives you a list of matching items from which to choose. Press Return, and whatever you chose opens. That's the same as Spotlight, but these programs go one better by learning your abbreviations for items, so you can, for example, type ps and open Adobe Photoshop. But you're not limited to just opening what you find; you can also do other actions. For example, if you type a friend's name, you can choose to send them an instant message, show their contact information, copy or paste their address or phone numbers, and more. LaunchBar (www.launchbar.com) is $20. QuickSilver is free (quicksilver.blacktree.com).

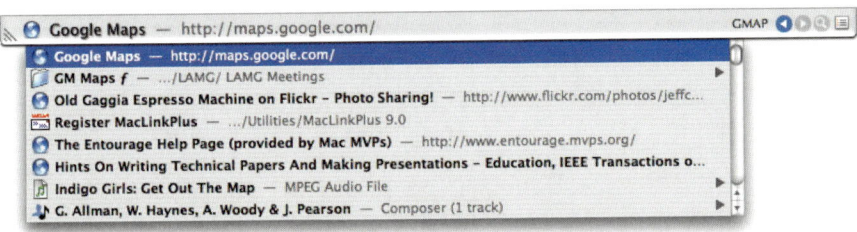

Finding a URL in my Safari bookmarks with LaunchBar.

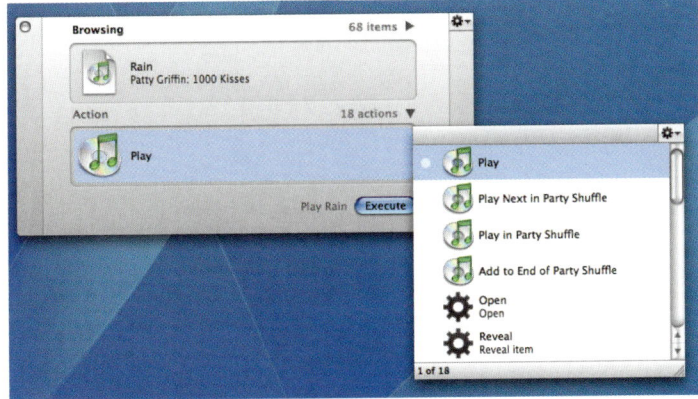

QuickSilver gives easy access to many actions for the selected item.

enhance file dialogs

Tiger brings some nice improvements to the Open and Save dialogs, as detailed in previous chapters. But they could still use a little help, and that's the job of Default Folder X, by St. Clair Software ($35, www.stclairsoft.com).

Default Folder X allows you to navigate more easily throughout your folders, by adding hierarchical menus in the Open and Save dialog's top menu. You can easily get to any folder on your hard drives in one selection.

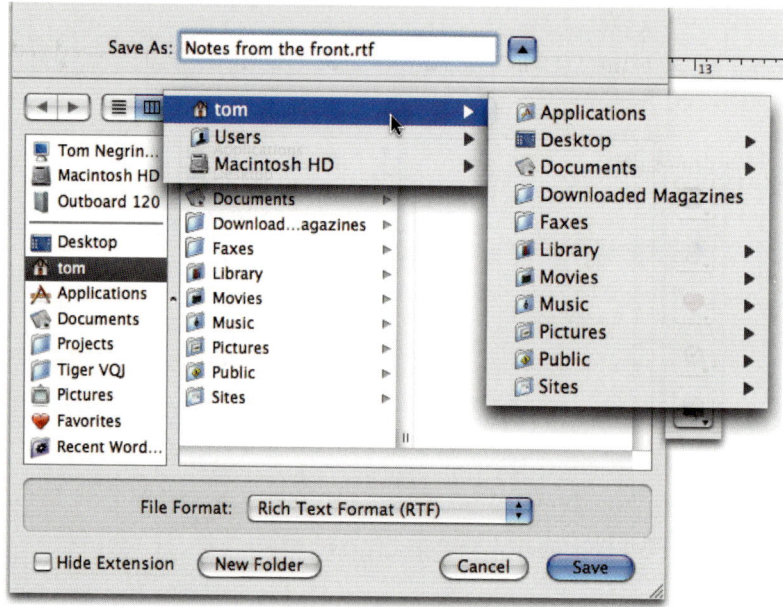

terrific additions for tiger

The program adds a toolbar to the right side of the Open and Save dialogs; the toolbar contains pop-up menus that allow you to create a new folder, rename a folder, get info, or trash a selected item, without leaving the file dialog. You can also set favorite folders, which is great for instantly jumping to a particular folder that you are using for a particular project. The recent folder pop-up menu keeps track of all the folders that you've used to save or open documents, so you can jump back to them. You can even assign shortcut keys to folders to jump to them instantly. You can also make the Open or Save dialog go to a folder in the Finder with a pop-up menu that shows you all of the windows you have open in the Finder.

Another great feature is that in Save As dialogs, you can click on the name of an existing file to copy its name to the Name box, so you don't have to retype the same or similar filenames.

Default Folder rebounds back to the last item that you selected in a folder, so when you go to reopen a file you had been working on, it's immediately available—you don't have to go search for it. And finally, you can set a default folder for each application. For example, you can set file dialogs in Word to always open to your Documents folder, and in iMovie to always jump to your Movies folder.

enhance the clipboard

The Clipboard has been an integral part of the Mac OS since 1984. So it's puzzling that more than twenty years later, you can only cut or copy one thing to the Clipboard at a time. Wouldn't it be better if you could copy a variety of text or pictures to the Clipboard, and then choose what to paste? You could store text that you frequently use in the Clipboard, and it would be ready to paste whenever you needed it. That's what iClip, from Inventive, Inc. ($20, www. inventive.us) and CopyPaste X from Script Software ($30, www.scriptsoftware. com) do. Both programs allow you to have multiple sets of clipboards, and each offers its own unique features. You can access the clipboards via your choice of palettes, a menu, or hotkeys.

iClip shows you the contents of its clipboards with a preview bubble.

Besides multiple clipboards, CopyPaste X provides a full text editor and a great feature called yType, which is a "typing accelerator." This fixes frequent misspellings or typos automatically ("adn" becomes "and"), lets you substitute abbreviations for boilerplate text ("bb" becomes "http://www.backupbrain.com"), and more. It's a big time saver.

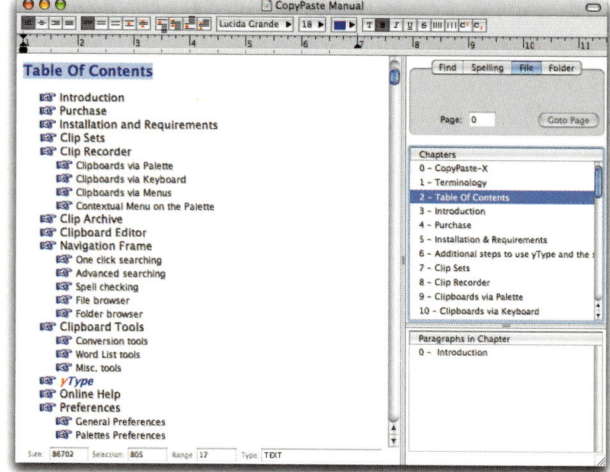

terrific additions for tiger

look in the grab bag

The programs in this section are ones that I think are terrific, but don't fall into a single category. I use all of these programs and utilities, and they're well worth your time to check them out.

The first pick is a plug-in for Safari that does something that Safari already does, but does it a lot better. One of the new features in Safari for Tiger is the ability to view PDF files right in the browser window. But the PDF Browser Plugin from Manfred Schubert (free; www.schubert-it.com/pluginpdf/) provides many more abilities than Safari, including the ability to show PDFs as individual or facing pages; split view, so you can look at two different parts of a document simultaneously; print and save the PDF; support for the PDF's table of contents; and support for links and text fields, so you can fill out PDF forms right in Safari.

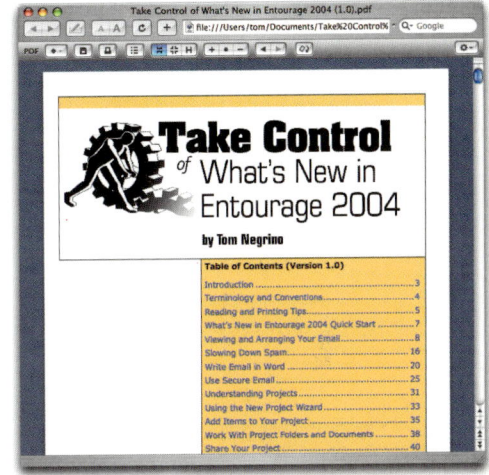

Do you use the Stickies application, or the new Dashboard Stickies widget? They're fine, but they're not very powerful. Instead, take a look at Sidenote, by Pierre Châtel (free; www.chatelp.org/?s=Sidenote). Sidenote is a drawer that hides at the side of your screen, showing only the bare edge of its window. When you move your mouse pointer over Sidenote, it slides out to reveal a window that can accept text that you type (or copy) into it, pictures, sounds, or video. The window has multiple pages, and entries are saved automatically. Like Stickies, you can change the note's font, style text, and its background color.

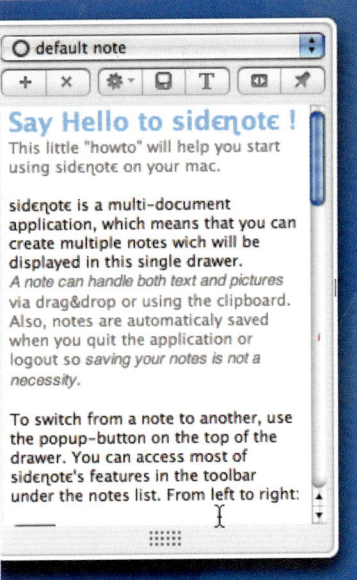

Many people rely on Lemkesoft's GraphicConverter ($30; www.lemkesoft.com/en/graphcon.htm) to edit images, convert images from one format to another, browse images, display slideshows, and much more. It's no Photoshop, but it's also a fraction of the price. Highly recommended.

If you're looking for a terrific text editor, look no further than Bare Bones Software's TextWrangler (free; www.barebones.com). It's perfect for people who need a much more powerful text editor than Apple's TextEdit, and for people who need to open and save files to remote servers via FTP.

Speaking of FTP, sometimes you need a good FTP (File Transfer Protocol) program to send and receive files from FTP servers. My favorite is the humorously named Cyberduck (free; cyberduck.ch). This terrific program supports regular and secure FTP and is very easy to use.

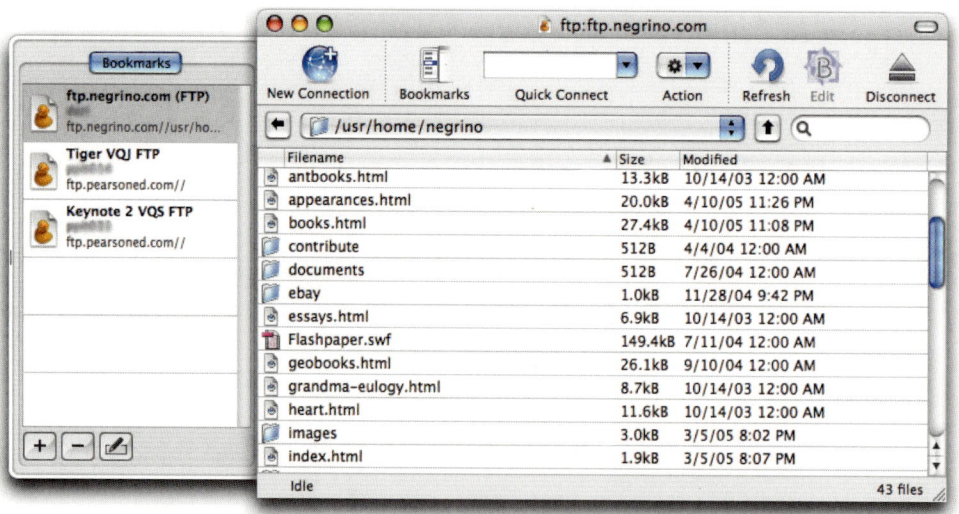

Lastly, here's a little goodie for laptop users. Apple's battery display takes up a bit too much of the menu bar on my PowerBook. SlimBatteryMonitor (free; www.orange-carb.org/SBM/) to the rescue! It's a replacement power gauge that has better display options than Apple's battery display.

extra bits

use a launcher p. 118

- Here is a tip, not for launching a program, but for switching between programs that you already have running. Press Command-Tab to bring up a floating window that shows all the icons for the currently open programs. Hold down the Command key, and press Tab repeatedly to move between programs. Release the keys to switch to the selected program. This feature was introduced in Mac OS X 10.3 Panther, but many people still don't know about it.

index

index

index

index

Ready to Learn More?